DADDY'S DIARY

THE ADVENTURES OF AN EVERYDAY FATHER

J. KEVIN MORRIS

Plain Sight Publishing
An Imprint of Cedar Fort, Inc.
Springville, Utah

ISBN 13: 978-1-4621-1166-4

Published by Plain Sight Publishing, an imprint of Cedar Fort, Inc.
2373 W. 700 S., Springville, UT 84663

Distributed by Cedar Fort, Inc., www.cedarfort.com

LIBRARY OF CONGRESS CATALOGING-IN-PUBLICATION DATA

Morris, J. Kevin (James Kevin), 1951-
Daddy's diary : the adventures of an everyday father / J. Kevin Morris.
pages cm
Includes bibliographical references and index.
ISBN 978-1-4621-1166-4 (alk. paper)
1. Morris, J. Kevin (James Kevin), 1951---Family. 2. Authors, American--21st century--Family relationships. 3. Fatherhood--United States. I. Title.

PS3613.O7725Z46 2013
813'.6--dc23
[B]

2012050249

Cover design by Rebecca J. Greenwood
Cover design © 2013 by Lyle Mortimer
Edited and typeset by Whitney A. Lindsley

Printed in the United States of America

10 9 8 7 6 5 4 3 2 1

For J. C.,
the world's greatest dad

PRAISE FOR

DADDY'S DIARY

"I devoured *Daddy's Diary* in one sitting. Don't know when I've spent a more pleasant afternoon reading. Wonderful stuff. Practical and poignant words of advice and wisdom for all dads—whether once, now, or wannabes. And sprinkled with more good one-liners than a week's worth of Jay Leno monologues."

—Robert Hamblin, professor of English, director of Center for Faulkner Studies, Southeast Missouri State University, and author of *This House, This Town: One Couple's Love Affair with an Old House and a Historic Town* and *Crossroads: Poems of a Mississippi Childhood*

"In his new book, *Daddy's Diary: The Adventures of an Everyday Father*, Kevin Morris uses wit, metaphor, and insight to make his personal stories of "daddyhood" absolutely relatable to you and to me and to daddies everywhere. It's Kevin's story, true; but as I laughed out loud one minute and welled-up the next, I felt in a very visceral way that it's mine too. As will you, I believe."

—Larson Bennett, marketing strategist, voice-over talent, and author of *Roaming Rhino Blog* and *Rhino Writes Blog*, www.rhinowrites.com.

OTHER BOOKS BY

J. KEVIN MORRIS

Strangely Normal: The Mostly True Tales of an Incurable Oddball

CONTENTS

ACKNOWLEDGMENTS

I acknowledge with appreciation Shersta Gatica, Angie Workman, Whitney Lindsley, Rebecca Greenwood, Rodney Fife, and other members of the Cedar Fort family who believed in my work enough to try this again.

I am grateful to Robert W. Hamblin and James P. Bell, who offered encouragement and helpful advice in the completion of this and other works; and to Larson Bennett and Erin McClellan for their time and generosity.

A most respectful and loving thank you to my father, J. C. Morris Jr., and my mother, Mildred Ruth Hamblin Morris, for teaching me to believe I could. And to my "other parents," Max Dale Raddatz and Joanne Seare Raddatz, for loving me as their own.

To my children, Anne, Kristopher, and Jeremy: thank you for enduring my bumblings and shortcomings, and for helping me make it to this side of the daddying years, smiling.

To my incomparable grandchildren, Jackson, Kaleigh, John, Ashton, Kaden, Brianna, Belle, Ryan, and Preslie: thank you for letting me continue to be a daddy, in new and wonderful ways.

And, as always, I am most especially grateful to my sweet Dianne for being my partner.

PROLOGUE

IN THE BEGINNING

To be a daddy, you've gotta have kids—in one way, shape, or form.

Goes without saying.

And it takes two to produce kids.

Also goes without saying. I mean, a daddy and a mommy must both be involved, somewhere along the line.

Well, OK. I grant that both polished and bleeding-edge technology can alter the traditional formula of *one daddy plus one mommy equals kiddos*. But I'm not gonna address any of that. For my purposes now, the traditional take on things will suffice.

As far back as my memory will take me, I wanted a family. You know. Wife. Kids. *Family*. In 1973 I met Dianne, the woman who would make it happen. The roads we'd traveled to our intersection had been crooked and forked, with several switchbacks and a U-turn or two. Hers had meandered through relationships that appeared to be right, in their day—and mine had seemed destined at times to end at other places before continuing on to intersect with Dianne's.

Simply said, she had relationships before we met, and so had I. Of course, that's the way it usually goes. After all, the only way to get to who you are is to go through who you were.

And who knows why things turn out as they do? We might argue till Phoenix is frigid whether any relationship is discovered according to our own travel plan or mercifully granted to us by some higher force giving us access to a perfect, intangible GPS that sends us down just the right roads to just the right intersection at just the right time. Or maybe it's all simply a matter of luck and coincidence.

Pick which position you'll defend. Just be advised that whichever you pick, some wisenheimer's gonna argue your choice. But whatever its etiology, one thing about a relationship's for dang sure: you'd better like the person you marry.

Yep, I said *like.* Not *love.* Oh, sure—*love* is the principle emotion that wants to be in the driver's seat here, and I'm not *about* to debate the role love plays in a marriage relationship.

Seems quite obvious that it plays an essential role.

That said, I'll confidently argue anyone who cares to step up to the challenge that *loving* someone without *liking* that someone isn't only *possible* but may be at the root of the highest divorce rate in the world. [*Social Irony Note:* The good news is, the United States divorce rate seems to be declining.[1] The bad news is that the rate may be because fewer people are bothering to marry.[2]]

Yep, you'd better *like* the one you marry, because . . . well, because when the children have flown the nest at last, only two people will remain.

The same two who started this whole thing.

NOTES

1. U.S. Census Bureau, *Statistical Abstract of the United States: 2012*, Table 1336.

2. Ibid., Table 63.

ONE

BEATLES AND FEELINGS

Life is brimming with feelings, and a feeling is an amazing thing. It's the powerful unseen force that influences opinion, inspires discipleship, persuades repetition, or condemns outright. A feeling filters our perception of something, allowing us to see certain of its parts clearly while obscuring others. Kinda like the Ben Franklin spectacles in Disney's *National Treasure*.[1]

I've had some pretty grand feelings in my life. While I know this doesn't single me out for medals or knighthood—I mean, who doesn't have feelings?—I've got a nickel that says my feelings can take your feelings.

And in the autumn of my life I've tried to rank-order the feelings of a lifetime. Yeah, that's right. *Rank-order* them. Likely, you haven't bothered to do that . . . well, unless it was a therapeutic assignment given to you by a mental health practitioner. If so, good on ya, mate. But I've done it, and without assignment.

First, let me just point out that it's no easy process, this rank-ordering feelings. I mean, it's a tad like trying to rank-order Beatles songs.

Allow me to explain.

I'm big into sixties music, and my family and friends know that about me. In fact, anyone who's had the (mis)fortune of speaking with me for longer than ten minutes knows that about me. And I can empty a fairly crowded room quicker than you can say *I love you, Alice B. Toklas* by taking just a few verbal steps down music memory lane—if the average age in the room's younger than fifty years, or if the bunch isn't, for whatever reason, into oldies music.

Be that as it may, I've come to terms with the loneliness of my obsession. I love my oldies—that's all there is to it. And I'll bet tweezers, turtles, or taffy that I'll be listening to a Gary Puckett song—as I've done every day since 1967—when I croak; no apologies.

I've been asked countless times—and about a batrillion books have addressed this very question—which Beatles song I think is the greatest ever. Talk about a question that's impossible to answer. No *way* can *any*one single out one lone Beatles tune as The Greatest. Just can't be done. Too many great ones to choose from. So the approach I've adopted over the years is to assign them, on a case-by-case basis, to a range.

Examples: "In My Life," "We Can Work It Out," "Nowhere Man," and "Here, There, and Everywhere" would be Top-Three songs. "Yesterday," "For No One," "Fool on the Hill," "Hey Jude," and "I Will"—Top-Five songs. "And Your Bird Can Sing," "If I Fell," and "I'll Follow the Sun"—Top-Ten songs.

I can assign the songs to a general range, but that's as precise as I can be.

[*Capacity Note:* Perhaps you noted that I listed more than

three Top-Three songs. That is correct, sir. I allow myself to assign more than three songs to my Top Three, more than five, to my Top-Five, and so on. Violates laws of mathematics, I know. But's it's the best way I know to assign a relative level of "topness"—I doubt that's a word—to the Fab Four's many great tunes.]

And the world's got the same problem, apparently. If you don't believe me, just check out the variance among the lists people have compiled to definitively rank-order Beatles songs. Heck, *no* one agrees with *any*one else.

[*Unequivocal Note:* When it comes to picking my favorite Gary Puckett song, I'm less confused, because it goes without saying: My favorite's every one he's ever done. But such perfect decisiveness is reserved for Mr. Puckett, and Mr. Puckett alone.]

So I rank-order feelings like I rank-order Beatles songs. And I share now three of my Top-Three feelings.

***

On my eleventh birthday, my family and I left the small town of Baldwyn, Mississippi, and headed for a new home in Orange County, Southern California. Fullerton, to be precise. My father had to teach in a public school for two years in order to acquire a necessary credential, and the earning power of a Mississippi teacher in 1962 was roughly equivalent to that of a panhandler on a skid row street corner. Yep, in 1962 a certified teacher in the Magnolia State pulled down a nation-low average of $3,560 per year, while California paid a nation-high $6,900.[2]

California, here we come.

We climbed into the spacious sedan we'd rented for the one-way trip and headed for legendary US Route 66, which would take us clear to California's San Bernardino Valley. That two-thousand-mile journey took me through cities and states and across deserts and prairies and over rivers and mountains I'd never dreamed I'd see.

When at last we rolled up and over the San Bernardino mountains and I got my first look at that valley sprawling majestically below, I was speechless.

What I *saw* was California—a new world that, as I imagined it, held unopened treasures of sight and sound and experience just waiting to be discovered by this transplanted eleven-year-old Mississippian. It was special, seeing this new land—but what I *felt* was even more special. Excitement, awe, expectation, suspense, wonder, curiosity, thrill—all these blended to create a singular emotion unlike anything I'd known up to that moment of my young life. Through the eye of that emotion, I saw my life sweeping down that fabled road to the new valley below, there to merge with another road that would lead to another road, and that road to another—and on and on, all roads in turn finally taking me, metaphorically and literally, to every single place I'd need to be, in order to realize what I was to become. And to do what I was to do.

That, right there—that was a Top-Three feeling.

***

Now, I've always liked girls. There's just no denying it. By way of preparing me, I suppose, to recognize The Right One when she crossed my path, I enjoyed boyfriend-girlfriend relationships from time to time, sprinkled timely—strategically, even—over the whole of my young life. And I've known some wonderful xx-chromosome types in my day. From the lovely girls of my childhood—Peggy, Bobbie, Emily, Rosemary, Linda, Sally—to those outstanding young ladies of my adolescence—Connie, Margo, Judy, Debbie—and on to Lucy and Jody, the near-miss relationships of my young adulthood. Yep, these were great people, every single one. Some of them can no doubt be credited with helping me make good decisions at certain critical points in my life—decisions that sent me down happy roads when I might as easily have stumbled onto harsher, sadder roads. Such is the power of genuine friendship.

My sincere thanks to each of them.

If I were telling this instead of writing it, here's where I'd sing a verse or two of the Hammond/David tune, *To All the Girls I've Loved Before*[3]—just to, you know . . . make my point. Good thing for you I'm writing.

Yep. The little misses on my list of girlfriends were lovely and special. And the ones with whom I've stayed in touch over the years are *still* lovely and special.

But when I met Dianne in 1973, I knew hers would be the last name on that list.

Okay, well . . . it took a minute for the thing to develop, that's true. Heck, I'm a guy, don't forget. That means I've got the emotional IQ of a trailer hitch, give or take a point. Gimme a break. I don't remember ever *asking* to be a guy. I just play the dang cards.

But despite the limitations of my defective emotional synapses, a relationship developed between Dianne and me—a relationship that seemed to be more than a little promising.

As I'd soon learn, it wouldn't disappoint.

Shortly after I met and dated Dianne for a time, I returned to my university studies, several hundred miles away. I left my new friend behind, with no official commitment between us. But after only two weeks, I knew what I wanted. And you can bet your last Dahnken's Diamond Showroom discount coupon I wasn't gonna wait till my Thanksgiving-holiday jaunt down to Orange County to get it.

Ma Bell was about to become my new best friend.

***

On September 10, 1973, I picked up the handset of the cherry-red model 2554 Western Electric telephone hanging on the kitchen wall and pushed the numbered buttons that would connect me with the Raddatz home in Placentia, California. My heart was in my mouth, my knocking knees were keeping time to a brisk John Philip Sousa march, and my lungs were shedding enough carbon dioxide to make the Black Forest light-headed. Physically, I qualified for intensive care. And *mentally*—well, while I listened to muffled rings and waited for someone to answer, thoughts raced through my mind in a way that's neurologically impossible. No, really. It's *impossible.* In a piece of respectable research, the following was put forward: "Above all else, this research shows with incontrovertible conclusiveness that, while documented and known to have actually occurred, it is neurologically, sensorially, and chemically impossible for the human brain—from the least capacious to the most—to simultaneously process multiple parallel thoughts, speaking in terms of both quantity and complexity, at the rate experienced by Mr. Morris on the evening of 10 September 1973."

I'm not gonna footnote a reference for the quote, however, because . . . well, because I made it up.

But if anyone had bothered to conduct that particular bit of research, I guaran-dang-TEE the same conclusion would've been reached.

By the time Dianne's mom, Joanne, picked up her ringing phone, I believe I'd enjoyed—my memory may be slightly blurred on this bit of detail, I'll grant—approximately twenty-seven quadrabazillitrillion rings. I had enough time anyway to briefly lose consciousness at least twice and chew three fingernails down to the first knuckles.

"Hello?"

"Uh . . . hello. Mrs. Raddatz?" I stammered. "This is Kevin calling. Kevin Morris. Is Dianne there?"

"Oh, hi, Kevin! How are you?"

"I'm fine, thanks. How are you?"

"We just couldn't be better. I think Nanny's around here somewhere. Hang on just a moment and I'll find her."

And another brief slip into unconsciousness.

After slightly less than four weeks' time—time dilation's an unfortunate product of sheer terror—I heard Dianne's sweet voice.

"Kevin, is that you?" She sounded happy, but at that moment I was so loopy I couldn't swear to the accuracy of any perception I might think I had.

"Yeah. Hey." I tried to echo her happiness but my tongue was approximately fourteen times its normal size, and my uvula was glued to the roof of my mouth, so who knows what feeling I actually conveyed. It wasn't fearlessness, I can tell you that.

What followed was a brief conversation consisting mostly of small talk. She was glad I was doing OK in school and I was liking the apartment and my roommates, and she'd been busy with this and that, and I was amazed she hadn't already found some handsome critter to replace me.

OK, so I didn't actually *express* that last thought. But I *had* it; you can bet the Great Carnac's bejeweled turban on that.

Eventually I came to the proverbial fork in the road and knew I had to pick my path. I gathered what pluck I could find, screwed my courage to the sticking-place, and prepared to face my emotional foe.

I'm not talking about Dianne. She wasn't my foe, emotional or otherwise. *Nerves.* I'm talking about *nerves.*

"I've been . . . uhh . . . doing just a . . . just a lot of . . . umm . . . a lot of thinking, and I think . . . umm . . . . I think . . . well, I mean . . . uhh . . . well, I was wondering if you'd . . . umm . . . if you'd . . . well, if you'd . . . uhh . . . marry me."

There. I'd done it.

"Yes, I will."

No pause. No hesitation. No clarifying question. No *maybe, but I'll have to think about it and get back to you.*

Well, at least I *think* there was no pause—but I remind you of my impaired perception of time. Maybe the answer came twenty-seven minutes after I asked the question and I was just too muffle-headed to know.

However long it took or didn't take, the answer was *yes.*

She said *yes.*

Wow.

With that one-syllable word, I saw my life once again as I'd seen it in my mind's eye on New Year's Day 1963, when I looked down at the San Bernardino Valley below and envisioned all the roads that would eventually take me where I was bound to be. Now I could see other highways reaching even farther beyond. In that moment, all the things I'd experience from that day forward, all the love and joy and challenge and sorrow and failure and opportunity that would be mine—all this appeared in a flash before my mind's eye, nearly as perceptible as the projected image of a movie. In that instant I knew the right thing had just happened and that because of it, other right things were gonna happen. My anxiety subsided, my mind cleared, and my focus sharpened. And all this combined into a most perfect feeling that paradoxically mixed hope with surety, excitement with composure, anticipation with patience.

That, right there—that was a Top-Three feeling.

***

So we got married, Dianne and I. Shortly after, we got pregnant. Night follows day.

See, to our thinking, having a baby was simply the next step to take after marriage. Just as countless other generations before us had done, we expected children to come. We hoped for children, counted on children. We didn't *plan them out*, as is often the case with young adults nowadays. Nope, no game plan or tactical strategy for us. Just dive right in.

Make no mistake. We were excited about having a child—about having child*ren*. Dianne was raised with six siblings—a large family, by modern standards. I was raised beside three siblings—a more modest household. The difference in the size of our parents' families notwithstanding, the two of us had long dreamed of having children of our own.

Now we wanted the reality.

And despite a bit of morning sickness for one of us and some mutual trepidation—this was, after all, a new and unfamiliar journey we were beginning—nothing thrilled us more than the thought of having a child. We were excited and humbled to think that we'd be facing the greatest responsibility of all: bringing into the world and raising a real, actual person.

We approached the end of a relatively unremarkable pregnancy—easy for *me* to say, I guess—and as the delivery date drew near, we were eager to welcome the little guy or gal that would be sharing quarters with us for a couple of decades. Of course, we'd no idea what flavor this little stranger was—in 1975 it wasn't common for parents to know the sex of the baby before the little rascal popped into the world and showed off its potential. Such mystery, by the way, led to many yellow- and green-painted nursery walls and lots of neutral-colored onesies and booties at baby showers. I mean, you just couldn't afford to invest a whole big bunch of money—which you didn't have, anyway—in a lot of pink, frilly stuff only to see a little boy come smiling out to greet you.

At last the delivery date was upon us. And whoever said it takes forty weeks for a baby to percolate's just full of wind, as far as we were concerned, 'cause the due date for this little critter came and went without notice.

Well, not *completely* without notice.

Dianne noticed.

And before long, I noticed too. I may be slow, but I'm eventual. At last it dawned on me that there was still a big lump where there should be none. Yep, Dianne's belly was beginning to look kinda like the south end of a northbound hippo. But bravely, day after day, my beautiful round sweetheart trudged on, hoping against hope that today would be The Day.

As the calendar rolled on, I grew more and more anxious. I mean, I was nervous as a democrat in the Utah State Legislature. Every day I'd go to my university classes and then to work in the evening, helping care for a group of eight young boys with multiple severe disabilities. I was constantly on alert for The Call, and I expected it to come at any minute. Heck, it just *had* to come soon. If things went on this way much longer, we'd be able to take the kid right from the delivery room to the admissions department of the nearest college and get it enrolled.

And don't think I didn't worry that Dianne would kick into labor while I was in a classroom, unreachable. I did. Oh, yeah, I did. Only other expectant fathers could possibly understand the twenty-four-seven agony that was mine as I continually hoped and prayed that the timing of my sweetheart's urgency would cooperate with my daily schedule and contain itself till I could be near a phone at work.

***

I'll bet everyone who's ever lived on this planet has known someone like the person I'm about to describe. Someone with no concept of the difference between *funny* and *mean*. No idea about when something (s)he thinks *oughta* be funny just flat *isn't*. No sense of timing. No mark of decency. No . . . No . . .

Well, no *brain*, as it were.

I'm talking about the kind of person who'd yell "fire!" in a crowded movie theater and just laugh and laugh as the weak and helpless were driven savagely to the soda-pop-sticky, bubble-gum-crusted floor and trampled senseless.

You know the one I'm talking about. You *know* you do.

Edith's the one I knew. She worked the evening shift with me. Nice enough, to be sure—and I liked her. But her top drawer wasn't quite closed, and she lived in her own special place.

I'd just brought my eight boys into the dorm area of the facility where I worked, to help them prepare for bed. After my good friends were showered, medicated as appropriate, properly suited for bed, and tucked in, I addressed the several assigned chores that had to be done before my shift ended.

As I exited the dorm area through the double door that led to an open commons where stood the mop and bucket I'd be using for my first chore, here came Edith—flying out of the main office just around the corner, headed right for me. She was wide-eyed and yelling at the top of her squeaky little voice, flailing arms carving the air madly.

"Kevin! Kevin! Phone call! HOSPITAL!"

In a heartbeat, I was mentally blank and physically incapable. It was as if all light suddenly vanished, my neurons refused delivery on any electricity, and every single muscle melted like butter in Death Valley. Familiarity with the English language evaporated into the ether, leaving behind only senseless babble. Within moments, my heart had proved that a rate of twenty bazillion beats per second doesn't necessarily mean death.

Summoning that last remaining ounce of strength and determination, I pulled myself together—more or less—and lurched spastically toward Edith, the town crier wannabe who was now bouncing up and down and clapping her hands as though she'd just seen Happy the Clown juggle twelve Easter baskets and drop only two of them. I was headed toward the office just the other side of the maniacal messenger, and the telephone awaiting me there.

But it was not to be a direct route. And there would be injuries along the way.

***

The first hitch to my adrenaline-fired betweetlement was that mop I mentioned and the bucket of gray water it was sticking out from. You know the rig—a big ol' four-wheeled metal bucket with a side wringer that squeezes out all the grunge the wet mop-head picked up on its last pass across a filthy floor. I slammed into the handle of that wringer, planting the seeds of a knee bruise that, tomorrow, would be worthy of media coverage—and there went the mop and the bucket, and all the bucket's lathery contents. A shimmering sheen of slippery suds now covered the floor, and I surfed the linoleum like a gremmie anglin' a gnarly North Shore heavy, arms thrashing to find balance and feet never going the same way twice in a row. I was all elbows and kneecaps, kinda like Sylvester in the movie

The Bishop's Wife, when, in ice skates for the first time ever, he steps onto the ice with Dudley and Julia.[4]

Down I went.

Sprawled on the floor, I was down but not out. I fought my way back to the vertical, determined to complete this pilgrimage to the sacred telephone. Feet slipping and sliding back and forth and forth and back like a cartoon character stranded on a slick spot, I finally captured enough traction to move more or less forward—slowly at first, and then, with momentum, faster than I cared to go. And even though I really and truly wanted to stop at the office door, momentum and slick soles teamed up against me and insisted that I just keep sliding right on past it and toward the dining room beyond, metal trash cans flying here and there as I slid.

And then I crashed to the floor again.

Back on my feet once more, I sloshed my way to the office door, grabbed its frame for anchor, and reached for the telephone on the desk in front of me.

The beige handset rested, quiet and undisturbed, on the base's switch hook.

There was no one at the other end of *this* line—you could bet your fractured left tibia on it.

And then the cackle. That crazy, explosive, shrill, fingernails-on-a-blackboard *heh heh heh heh heh heh*, just over my right shoulder.

Edith.

It took a moment for me to realize I'd been had, and well. Yep, she got me good with that one. Under more ordinary, non-life-and-death circumstances, perhaps I'd have found Edith's prank creative. Well executed. Even funny, maybe.

Not today.

And other friends nearby who'd witnessed the whole thing

were equally unimpressed. They weren't laughing. Nope, not laughing at all. They saw the cruelty of this little prank and simply did *not* find it funny. Truth be told, the only semblance of laughter to be heard was Edith's twitter, and even that nervously subsided as a menacing crowd gathered about her.

As I caught my breath, regained my composure, and searched in vain for an errant bit of Mellaril or other phenothiazine that I could put to use, the mob closed in on the prankster. And the last I saw of Edith, she was headed briskly toward downtown, one shoe on and one shoe off, stealing an occasional over-the-shoulder glimpse of the pitchfork-toting, torch-bearing, fist-shaking, threats-shouting crowd hot on her sadistic little heels.

Maybe they caught her. I don't know.

***

Now a full four—yep, I said *four*—weeks after Dianne's due date, she and I found ourselves at her regular appointment with the doctor. The two of us listened intently as he assured us that the little intrauterine rascal was doing fine. Nothing to worry about here, he insisted. All was well, he promised.

"Well, all may be well from *your* point of view," I explained to the way-too-patient ob-gyn, "but from my wife's point of view things are dragging on just a bit long. And I'm agreeing."

The man with gloved hands and standard-equipment smile tried to placate this aggravated dad, but I was having none of it. What with worrying day and night without relief and nearly killing myself getting to a crank phone call, I'd had enough. E-N-O-U-G-H. *Enough.* And as my dad is wont to say, enough's enough, and too much is a hound dog's bait. In the boldness of my misery, I tersely explained to the doc that his choice was simple: he was gonna admit Dianne to the hospital and give nature a hand with this thing, or I was gonna give my very tired bride thirty cc of castor oil and take her on a winding ride through the nearby canyon.

At 6:00 p.m. we were admitted to the maternity unit at the local hospital. Before you could say, *How's the family?* Dianne was prepped, positioned, and panting.

Now, I'd accompanied my baby's mama to those Lamaze birthing classes during the final weeks of pregnancy—but if I learned anything at all, it was failing me now. Shoot, I couldn't remember which side I parted my hair on, let alone any finer points of the principles of continuous labor support or spontaneous pushing in upright or gravity-neutral positions. I was panting as much as Dianne was, and being about as useful as teats on a boar. Mostly I was just performing the simple duty of aggravating my wife in her misery. And I do mean *misery.* Heck, this intrepid lady was doing the whole gig naturally, with no spinal block or medication or even a merciful head thump. She was hurting. Brave through it all, to be sure—and complaining far less than I'd complain if roles were reversed. But hurting. And every word of intended comfort I could manage seemed more a dagger than a rose petal.

Now, in childbirth, women may lay rightful claim to the greatest physical pain available to humans, but I'm here to set the record perfectly straight on this thing. Here's the true skinny: whatever level of physical pain Mom reaches during childbirth, in many ways it pales in comparison to the special agony Dad feels.

See, we males are exposed to certain indoctrination from the day we're born till the day we croak—indoctrination that, whether a function of nature or of tradition, teaches us that we're to be Lord Protector of the Realm. Keeper of the Castle. Protector Familiare, as it were. Our lot is to protect. To defend.

To keep pain, insult, injury, misery, and danger from the doorstep of our loved ones—and, above all, from the doorstep of the mother of our children. We're prepared to face trouble, to risk peril, to go to battle—to lay ourselves at the very altar, if necessary, to prevent or ease her suffering.

But here, at this moment of childbirth, seeing the unique and perhaps unequaled suffering of our most beloved—when what we want more than anything in the world to do is help and ease—we can do nothing.

Powerless.

Now, you wanna talk about pain. There it is. *That's* the *ultimate* pain—but only a father can experience it. Only a father can understand it.

And what do we get in return for this silent agony born of devotion?

"Get away and never touch me again."

See, dads don't just get to suffer in silent helplessness as our sweethearts labor. Nope, we get a little something extra. We get to be the whipping boy—to shoulder the blame for every ouch, every pant, every needle, every contraction, every *push-no-wait-don't-push*. Now, I seem to remember both Mom and Dad being in the vicinity when the decision to make this little critter was reached, but never mind that now. Apparently the whole sordid deal is Dad's fault. And this succinct but effective dressing-down isn't simply a matter of words. It's words served up with a growl that can take a daddy to his knees, and a soul-searing *coup d'oeil* that can send him screaming into the night.

Such was the emotional venue in which I found myself in the wee hours of the morning, October 14, 1975.

***

Just at the very moment when I felt at once perfectly sympathetic, utterly helpless, emotionally saturated, and finally useless, there she was.

Anne.

The lovely resolution of an ironic conflict between Mom's ability and willingness to suffer physically and Dad's capacity and determination to endure the assault of traitorous emotions.

And then . . .

The First Cry. A soft but keen racket, at once blaring and perplexingly pleasant. A sound unlike anything I'd ever heard—unlike anything I'd ever imagined I *might* hear. A simple angelic intonation that chucked audible darts in my direction, piercing my heart and my spirit in ways I'd have sworn were impossible.

In that moment, I saw my life continuing yet farther down those life highways I'd envisioned before, on toward the next stretch of tomorrows beyond. But something was different. I sensed that my road, this time, wouldn't simply merge with another.

This time, it would find an interchange.

Behind the prophecy of her cry, I saw my newborn daughter's life moving forward too, shadowing mine for a time on my road, then veering with certain intent onto its own directed path—a path running parallel to mine, separate. And in that separation I saw—no, *felt*—the continuation of everything I'd ever wanted, everything I'd ever valued, everything I'd ever held to be important. I sensed the ultimate realization of all that should be and would be, unreachable by me on my own path.

But reachable by my daughter, on hers.

In a beat, my heart seemed all but silenced, so intense the meeting of relentless, wonderful emotion and pure, indescribable vision.

And that, right there—that was . . .

Well, I was gonna say *a Top-Three feeling*. But wait a minute, if you don't mind, while I argue with myself just a tad.

Yeah, I know. I said the best I could do was assign a general level of "topness"—nope, still not a word—to my feelings, but now that I've written these last few thoughts, I may be persuaded to change my thinking here.

I mean, this first cry of my first child, now . . . well, it's hard to say that what I felt when I heard it was more powerful or inspiring than what I felt when I saw California for the first time, or more beautiful or important than what I felt when I heard Dianne say yes. But something about this new, unexpected, inexplicable affect set it apart from the others.

See, as it washed over me like pure sparkling rainwater spilling over the rim of a soaked-full oak barrel onto rich dark earth below, I intuitively understood that this tremendous feeling was only the first of others of its kind to follow. Couldn't quantify or name them at the time, of course, but I knew they were coming, sure as Mister Green Jeans's pants aren't blue. Yep, I'd get to enjoy this same thrill again and again through the years to come.

I'd learn twice more that I was to be a father and, with their mother, hear the first cries of my sons, Kristopher and Jeremy, just as I heard Anne's. I'd see all three of them grow into people who would learn and love and do much good. I'd see them marry special people and raise their own families.

I'd learn at least nine times that I was to be a grandfather. I'd be beside my wife and my children as grandchildren came, and, good Lord willing, I'd see that next generation also grow into people who would learn and love and do much good. I'd see them marry special people and begin raising their own families.

And, with an additional measure of grace, I'd be beside my wife and my children and my grandchildren as great-grandchildren came. If not granted sufficient time to see this generation full-grown, perhaps enough to see the beginning of some marvelous journeys.

As that first cry of my first child settled warmly about me, I felt—no, *knew*—that I'd enjoy this most special joy over and over again, through as many years as I might be graciously allowed.

And that, right there—that wasn't simply a Top-Three feeling.

That, my friend, was the greatest feeling of all.

NOTES

1. *National Treasure*, directed by Jon Turteltaub (Burbank, CA: Walt Disney Pictures, 2004).

2. M. Udall, in *Congressman's Report, March 31, 1962—Arizona's Public Schools—How Well Are We Doing?* March 31, 1962, accessed July 15, 2012, http://www.library.arizona.edu/exhibits/udall/congrept/87th/620331.html.

3. Julio Iglesias and Willie Nelson, "To All the Girls I've Loved Before," music by Hal David, produced by Albert Hammond, on *1100 Bel Air Place* (New York: Columbia Records, 1984).

4. *The Bishop's Wife*, directed Henry Koster (Hollywood: Samuel Goldwyn Company, 1947).

TWO

BABY FOOD AND GROOMING

A lot of the time, dads are out of the house. They're working here, working there, running this or that errand, playing basketball with the boys. Whatever. They're *out*.

And that's a shame too, 'cause the real action's not found in the office or out on the streets or on the basketball court. The real action's found where the kids are.

At least that's how I found it to be.

I'm sad to say—but I bet I could prove it in a court of law—that Dad's absence from the nursery is sometimes—I said *sometimes*—a calculated thing, especially in Baby's first months when the duties of childcare can be a bit gruesome. Not every Tom, Dick, and Cletus is eager—or even *willing*, for that matter—to throw himself into the messy, grungy tasks of baby-care.

But let's be fair about this thing. I don't know whether the phenomenon's DNA-based or just more of that gender-based tradition that's been given some unspoken, consensual social okeydokey. Whatever the etiology, it seems that your average dad—*absit iniuria verbis*—simply doesn't have the stomach for a lot of what goes on in and around the nursery.

And who could blame us. Shoot, most of it's just plain *gross.*

Like, diapers. Those rotten things are more often than not filled with some foreign substance that would better be miles away. And food—I mean, how about that pureed whatever and strained whatchamacallit and blended whatsis and the like, almost none of which actually gets to Baby's inside and a great deal of which gets on Baby's—and Baby's feeder's—outside. Then there's that silly nose to be dealt with. Shoot, I don't know what all that stuff is that gets stuck up inside there or sometimes comes *out* of there, but it's just better ignored.

Plenty of stuff for a new dad to get into, in Baby's first few days and weeks and months—especially when you consider that he's probably still recovering from the injuries he sustained when he passed out in the delivery room.

Okay. So Dad gets a little help from Mom from time to time. Wink, wink. But sometimes his number gets called in the huddle and he's gotta face that defensive line head on.

Now, I've ducked my share of daddy duties, so I don't claim to be the Number One Primo Dad of the Universe. That'd be as bad as claiming I invented the Internet, and *that* could lead to a war of wits with Mr. Gore. What I *can* say and defend is that I brought unusual experience and skills with me on my maiden journey into daddydom—skills and experience that were the difference between getting a repulsive task done and hightailing it for the nearest travel agent.

Take those diapers I mentioned.

***

Shortly after Dianne and I returned to the university to continue my studies in '74, I took a part-time job at a residential facility for people with disabilities. At the time, more than a thousand individuals lived there—babies, toddlers, children, adolescents, adults, seniors—all of whom had disabilities ranging from severe to hardly noticeable. It was essentially a small city, this Training School, and its buildings and programs were organized by age, gender, level and type of disability, medical conditions, and behavioral disorders.

I ended up working as a psychologist there, but I began my ten-year stint as a part-time aide in the deaf-blind program. The ten young people who were served in that program ranged in age from eight years to the mid-teens, give or take. In those days, federal funding for deaf-blind programs was generous enough for a one-child-to-one-staff ratio, while in other Training School programs that ratio was maybe eight or ten to one. I worked evenings assisting an eight-year-old boy.

Hector was a great kid. He had a profound intellectual disability, no vision, little hearing, and no speech—but the guy's personality was to die for. I'd say it was cute, but then I'd have to explain to my grandsons why I'd use such a girly word. In the Morris family a guy simply doesn't use the word *cute*.

Be that as it may. Hector had a cu . . . I mean, a magnetic personality that drew a caregiver in like a black hole sops up space stuff. But to go along with his challenges in cognition, speech, vision, and hearing, the little man's self-help skills weren't what you'd expect at his age. Couldn't dress himself. Couldn't feed himself. Couldn't use the toilet by himself. He needed someone to help him do these things, and to teach him to do them as well as possible.

That's where I came in.

Most of the self-help shticks I had to do didn't cause me much grief, but then there was that toileting thing. To say that changing Hector's diaper wasn't the funnest thing I'd ever done in my young life would be like pointing out that Gary Puckett can sing: both are obvious. But it was part of my job, this diaper changing, and I did as I was assigned. In fact, even though I worked mostly with little Hector, from time to time I changed the diapers of older folks too.

Strangely, it didn't take long for me to desensitize. Before you could whistle a bar of "What in the World's Come Over You," I was washing a dirty diaper in the toilet with my left hand while eating a peanut butter sandwich in my right.

Now, the diapers we used back then weren't like the ones today—you know, the nice, neat, leak-proof, custom-fitted, *haute couture* disposables with pretty print designs and sticky-tape fasteners. Nope, these puppies were cloth. Plain, colorless, styleless cloth squares that had to be folded just so and pinned just right. And they could soak clear through, so they had to be covered by a pair of plastic protective panties if there'd be any hope of spontaneous nurturing. Every single nasty one of those reusable things—diapers, not babies—had to be washed out in the toilet and then kept in some kind of hamper till washday. A strangely aromatic hamper.

And the Training School didies weren't exactly what you'd call petite. Those suckers were big enough to house a bum the size of Cleveland. Heck, one of 'em could've doubled as a pup tent if you happened to get stranded in the wild. And the pins that secured those unwieldy monsters were eighty yards long. If you missed or overshot your target and ran the pointy end of one of those things under a fingernail or into the palm of your hand, people three counties away knew about it. And under a fingernail or into your hand's *always* where the dang thing went 'cause we put a hand between the diaper and the bootie while we pinned, just in case.

Oh . . . just . . . OUCH.

[*Generalization Note:* This pinning skill would've come in real handy back in '69 when I was trying to attach that unobliging orchid to Lucy's prom gown or that uncooperative carnation to Debbie's homecoming dress, that's for sure. You can't tell me those girls wouldn't have enjoyed the dances a lot more without those inconvenient tourniquets.]

The white cotton squares—well, they started out white, anyway—that Dianne and I put on our babies' cute little bottoms weren't nearly as big as the Training School version, but they still required pins. *Smaller* pins, yeah, but pins. And although a poke from one of these regular fasteners didn't hurt near so badly as when you impaled yourself on one of those Training School behemoths—think hand grenade versus atomic bomb—it still hurt like the dickens. You can bet your major medical deductible on that.

To put it mildly, by the time I'd faced the first dreaded dirty diaper of my *leet-tle* tiny baby daughter, I was already a veteran of some pretty extreme action. Heck, I'd enjoyed surprises that would've made Clive Barker and John Carpenter and Brian De Palma hold hands and seek the shelter of a mother's arms. So when I looked at my sweet baby Anne's work for the first time, I kinda went, "Is this it? Is that all there is?" Shoot, there wasn't anything in that diaper worth taking notice of, and certainly nothing to get my knickers in a twist. I mean, once you've gotten used to trudging hip-deep in the river, you're not bothered much by a puddle.

So here's the upshot to this diaper-changing thing: while lots of first-time dads my age were stressing and wincing and gagging and complaining and screaming into the night about having to deal with this—*eeewwww*—mess, to me it was a tiptoe through the tulips.

***

Sometimes I hate writing.

I mean, I get all passionate and sure about something and then write about it with exclamation points as though it's some great eternal truth, irrefutable and unchangeable—and then with the very next thought I find myself arguing with what I just wrote.

Example.

I claimed earlier that I brought special experience to bear as I adjusted to being a dad, and that the experience served to make all my daddy duties doable.

I may have lied just a tad. Exaggerated, at least.

See, it's absolutely true that my work at the Training School inoculated me against the *Oh-My-Holy-Heck-There's-No-Way-I'm-Getting-Near-That-Dang-Diaper* virus that infects most new dads. But the daily task of osterizing food for some of the people we served there did ab-so-lutely *nothing* to desensitize me to the disgusting food my own toothless little critters required.

Heck, I'm probably just plain wrong in even calling it *food*.

Maybe it's just *stuff*.

Whatever you call the substance in that little glass bottle-slash-jar, I never liked it. Never accepted it. Refused to taste it. R-E-F-U-S-E-D. *Refused*.

There's something just flat unholy about strained foo . . . I mean, strained *stuff*. No way in this world could the Lord have intended that carrots or rutabaga or eggplant be pounded into a paste before getting eaten. Or peas. Or peaches, pears, or plums. Heck, these things come out of the ground or off the tree as solid properties—and that's how they should be eaten.

Yep, these things are supposed to be chewed, not slurped.

Applesauce may be an exception, but let's not dwell on that.

As for ready-to-mix cereals . . . well, don't even get me started. That stuff's just plain awful. Terrible. Icky. But I'll grant it one single saving grace: If I broke a chair arm or a table leg, I just pulled out a box of rice cereal, dumped a bit into a bowl, added a dash of H_2O, applied it to the wooden arm or leg, and voila! Broken furniture repaired. Worked better than Elmer's.

[*Point-Taken Note:* The trademarked name, Pablum, derives from the Latin *pabulum*, meaning *foodstuff.* I believe I just suggested that all these baby concoctions were more *stuff* than *food*. Point: Kevin.]

And it should be just plain illegal to puree meat of any kind. It's a distasteful practice and an insult to the critter that gave its all for our sustenance. The disgusting thought of sucking chicken or turkey or beef through a straw should bring any right-thinking adult human to its knees, and usually does—but we don't blink at spooning gobs of that strained critter into the hapless mouths of helpless young'uns or lose a minute of sleep for having done it.

Yeah, that strained and blended stuff I was forced to feed my kids was something horrific, if you ask me. And I always found it amazing to see just how many kinds of food could be thrown together under one roof. Roasted Butternut Pomegranate Squash Delight. Apple Bacon Pumpkin Pot Roast Casserole. Vegetable Soy Lentil Green Bean Stew. Baked Alaskan Halibut Avocado Supreme. Gourmet Parsnip Eggplant Zucchini Surprise. I mean, who went to sleep at night and suffered the nightmares that led to such concoctions? Kinda brought to mind what Andy Warhol's sketchpad might've looked like after a no-holds-barred sixties weekend. It was all enough to make you wanna kick the first marketing executive you ran across.

I wouldn't have touched a bite of any of it, even if you'd threatened me with twenty-seven straight hours of Tupperware sales presentations.

Now, I suppose I might argue with myself just a smidgen if we're talking about the desserts that trickled down my young'uns' gullets. They were OK. Not *all* desserts, mind you. I mean, I found absolutely nothing appetizing about a sweet potato banana mash, or a chunky avocado delight, or a cucumber melon puree. When I think about those obscene concoction, I find myself sprinting to the bathroom to dry-heave for about a week—yep, even now, more than thirty years after the last spoonful of the revolting rubbish disappeared into the open mouth of my youngest.

But pudding, now. For me, that was a slightly different story. With Baby's version of pudding you could make a case for edible. See, baby pudding's mostly like real pudding. It's the texture it's supposed to be. There's no farm-grown pudding plant that gets pulled from the ground or plucked from a limb to be pureed or whipped or beaten into something it doesn't wanna be. Unlike strained veggies and blended fruits and pureed meats, baby food pudding doesn't ooze from the wicked bowels of an abused Cuisinart as some disastrously changed, unthinkable horror-of-a-mush. It is what it's supposed to be.

Okay, so with little sugar or added salt and what have you, it's a bit bland. I'll concede that. Still, unlike the strained turnips or blended turkey or chunky-whatever delight, I found the baby food version of pudding to be edible, and I never had much trouble facing the task if I was, for whatever reason, called on to taste it.

But no matter what type or flavor of substance I fed—make that *tried to feed*—to my babies, there was trouble.

***

Everyone that ever traveled the path of public education enjoyed a substitute teacher from time to time, I suppose. I know I did. And I can't remember a single one of those unfortunates that escaped the classroom unscathed. The poor souls always paid a price for having the gall to be community-minded enough to cover for an absentee teacher. It was largely the sub's own fault, though, if you ask me. Heck, the rent-a-mentor just showed up, figuring that we students would know what lesson was to be taught that day and what page the lesson was on. And foolishly expecting that we'd have the maturity to actually tell the truth about that lesson—or about anything else, for that matter.

But we always had our own agenda. Yep, to us this sub was nothing more than a *victime expiatoire,* doomed to suffer horribly at our hands. The moment we heard, "Okay, kids, so where did we leave off in our math book yesterday?" we knew that sub didn't have the first clue about the first thing. We were in total and complete control.

Perhaps my babies couldn't plan as structured and premeditated an attack as we high school students mounted against our substitute teachers, but make no mistake: from the high chair, the little rascals were in control.

Cathedra mea, regulae meae. My chair, my rules.

And the moment my little darlings saw Daddy, not Mommy, sit down to face them in the high chair, a single thought occupied their contrary little craniums:

Game on.

I suppose there are conditions less suited to the DNA structure of a guy than facing a six-month-old in a high chair, armed with only a jar of baby food and a baby spoon.

But none springs to mind.

From the moment I cracked the seal on that jar till I telephoned the on-call dispatcher at Fred's Flood and Disaster Recovery Services, there was nothing but tightly closed lips, leaking mouths, volcanic oral sprays, *haishu uke* or *awase uke* karate blocks, and blobs of varying size and consistency flying in every direction.

I don't know just how many muscles exist in a human baby's jaw-mouth-lips configuration, but I do know that my little critters could contract every single one of 'em at precisely the same moment, at will. And nothing short of Ol' Jeb's Blasting Powder could open that dang oral cavity enough to insert a baby food–laden spoon.

And if by the grace of some loving, compassionate Higher Force I happened to catch a fleeting glimpse of an opening and mustered the speed to get the spoon into the tiny crevice before those lips clamped shut again, it was only a matter of time—fractions of a decibillionth of a micro-nanosecond—before whatever I shoved in came back at me with a vengeance.

Splatter that would've made a Halloween haunted house decorator proud.

And while that was bad, I'm not sure it was worse than a disgusting tactic of baby-feeding that I was forced to use, if Baby was to get any nutrients at all. I didn't invent the tactic, but I had no choice but to use it—as offensive as it was to my guyness.

The ol' *scrape-it-up-after-Baby-spits-it-out-and-shove-it-back-in* tactic.

You know what I'm talking about. You spoon a bit of food and, with a piece of rare luck and maybe a minute or two of *airplane-into-the-hangar*, Baby actually lets the spoon enter the mouth. But then that law takes effect—the unwritten law or code of baby dining that forbids Baby from swallowing any bite of food completely the first time around. And after a brief moment on the palate, out comes the unwelcome stuff, hanging from every lip dimple you see. Then you scrape up the oozing surplus with the spoon and shove it in again. With this second effort, another tiny bit of it makes it down the gullet, but the rest of it . . . yep, out it squirts again.

Spit it, scrape it, shove it.

Shampoo. Rinse. Repeat.

Over and over again. Till it's all in, and in for keeps.

Just before the onset of puberty, I'd sent every last bite of strained stuff to the Belly Motel—where it was already conspiring to make me pay again, later—and was ready to serve dessert. But by now, all my physical, emotional, and mental capacities were drained like a Bedouin's camel-skin water bladder after a desert road trip gone bad. So I'd just stand back and indifferently chuck spoonfuls of pudding or cherry cobbler or chunky avocado delight in Baby's general direction, hoping some of it found an open mouth or at least landed somewhere on Baby's body and made its way to the inside through some kind of super-osmosis.

It was *not* a pretty sight when I fed my babies.

Keep in mind that none of this happened when Mommy fed the babies. Nope, the little tykes would be hungry, cooperative, and happy as a doggone clam when Mommy was on duty. Sometimes they'd even politely touch a neatly folded napkin to the corners of their mouths after a bite of food.

The horrors were reserved for Daddy, the substitute feeder.

And ten-ish years later, I'd at last learned compassion for every substitute teacher my cohorts and I ever sent screaming into the night, waving a ruler in one hand and a dictionary in the other and shouting, "I *am* a teacher! I *am* a teacher!"

***

Once upon a time in '69, when I was studying at—make that, *attending*—college, I was having some weird discussion with my dorm-mate and best friend, Scott, about lips and noses.

Yep, I said *lips and noses*. I *told* you it was a weird discussion.

Maybe we were reviewing yesterday's Zoology 100 classroom presentation about the human anatomy. Maybe we'd seen some girl whose incredibly gorgeous lips and nose had gotten our attention. Maybe Scott had just punched me out and we were assessing the damage. Who knows why a couple of college freshmen would discuss lips and noses.

But that's what we were doing.

To be more precise, we were considering the little dimple-slash-cleft between the nose and the upper lip. I'd never known the thing's name, or even that it *had* a name. But Scott knew stuff like that. He informed me that it's called the *philtrum*.

With that, I figured I was prepared to leave this world at any time, sure I'd learned everything worth learning. But then Scott asked if I knew what the philtrum was for, and I realized I still had one important thing left to learn. No, I didn't know what the thing was for, I told him.

"Well, it's a little trough that funnels all that stuff that runs out a kid's nose," he explained.

Hmmm.

I've carried that . . . that . . . well, I *thought* it was a *fact* around with me for forty-three dang years. And I guess I suffer from a deplorable lack of curiosity because I only just now researched the thing to see if what Scott told me was true.

Apparently, it wasn't.

Most of what I read suggests that the philtrum's function is obscure and probably unrelated to eating or speaking or any other useful action. But though it may have no function, the dang thing's *there*, isn't it—so it stands to reason that *someone* would associate it with *something*.

And someone did.

Seems the ancients believed the little weirdness had something to do with *love*. Seeing that the word comes from the ancient Greek *philtron*, one might be persuaded that they were right. Depending on which definition blows your skirt up—and I can't tell you which, if any, is correct, 'cause I just never got around to taking that class in ancient Greek—the word *philtron* means *to love* or *to kiss* or *love charm* or *love potion* or *love incantation*. In any case, the similarity in the various definitions suggests that a word derived from *philtron* would more likely be associated with amour than with post-nasal drip.

And now I find myself wondering what other erroneous info Scott supplied over the years.

The irony here is that even though Scott wasn't correct, he may not have been completely wrong. I mean, you have only to check out the upper lip of any runny-nosed toddler to know that the philtrum—its weirdness and possible connection to love notwithstanding—sometimes does just what Scott said it does.

And in my nursery experience, both that philtrum and the nose it was connected to got a constant workout.

***

At first, it's innocent enough. I mean, the little newborn critter's nose just isn't all that big. Couldn't imagine it being much trouble.

The problem was, Mom never wanted to let anything in, on, or around Baby's nose alone. Heck, I was just fine with a little splotch of this or that here or there, as long as I didn't have to touch it. Didn't seem to me that such a small detail called for any complicated strategy—or even action, for that matter. I'd just ignore the foreign-but-if-it-leaves-me-alone-I'll-leave-it-alone matter, hoping, I guess, that the little piece of whatever-it-was would grow so big it'd fall out all by itself, sooner or later. Then I'd just kick it aside, and that would be that.

But Mom insisted that we deal with the stuff. I always figured it must be some kind of Mothers Union violation to fail to take immediate action against nose matter, but I don't know.

And there was even a dang tool for dealing with it.

We had this blue poly-something suction bulb thingy with a long pointy spout and a big fat hollow belly that was used to vacuum out Baby's nose. You'd depress the bottom of the monster's hollow belly with your thumb, then stick the pointy end straight up the little nostril. When you released the bulb's bottom it'd just *sssssssuck* out everything from inside the nose that wasn't permanently attached or of use to the baby. At least you *hoped* that's all it sucked out.

I hated to use the thing, but not for the reasons you might think, probably. I mean, the sound of that suction was grody, to be sure. And the whole procedure just never went over very well with the kid, which usually meant a minor wrestling match that led to crying and yelling and shrieking and all that kind of thing.

Sometimes the baby got upset too.

But the main reason I hated using this vacuum-sucky-thingy was that I was just grossed out to the max when I pondered what was *inside* that dang hollow bulb after sucking out Baby's nose a bazillion times. So grossed out, in fact, that I developed *nosegunkaphobia*. This is a little-known but terribly severe condition that can seriously impair a dad's ability to groom his child properly. To be more descriptive, nosegunkaphobia's an irrational fear that the blue vacuum-sucky-thing's gonna burst in your hand mid-suck and release from the depths of its bowels the most disgusting crud imaginable, which then shape-shifts into an unnameable entity of vicious disposition and carries you off to Never Never Nose Land.

It never happened, but it *could* have. It COULD have, I tell you.

***

So whether he's suppressing the gag reflex while changing a diaper he'd rather not face, or drowning in some unholy strained substance that's supposed to be going into his young'un's mouth but mostly isn't, or using a scary *objet de curiosité* to groom the little critter's nose, Daddy's got his hands full with a baby, if he's available and up to the challenge.

Too bad some fathers opt instead for the downtown office or the conveniently evasive errand or the basketball court. Like I said, the real action's found where the kids are.

Coincidentally, that's where real dads are found too.

THREE

HOUSES AND COMMITMENTS

It seems that a father's responsibility, in the main, is to provide and protect. Heck, *some*body's gotta make sure there's enough moola flowing in and out of the kitty to keep everything copacetic on the home front, and *some*body's gotta figure out ways to make sure there's a home with a front in the first place.

Not that any of it's an individual effort, mind you. Certainly it's not. But if the buck's gotta stop somewhere, it might as well be with Dad, I think.

Still, in the overall picture of a family household, Dad's end-of-the-buckness is a bit of a technicality. What's required is an attitude of teamwork between husband and wife, where possible, that mustn't be weakened by egos or gender stereotypes or anything else. It's gotta be strong. Resilient. Nonnegotiable. It's gotta have the energy to plow through a mile-wide challenge and come out stronger on the other side.

***

Dianne and I married in Southern California in '74 and then returned right away to the university to continue my education.

Right after that, we became poor.

Poor—an understatement of grand proportions. I mean, yeah, we'd worked hard and saved our pennies for tuition and living expenses ever since we'd gotten engaged, and we thought we'd saved sufficient for our student-living needs—but that's how much we knew. After moving into a spanking-new apartment that cost way more than we'd budgeted—we had no choice, but that's another story—we were already batting on a rather sticky wicket.

Dianne found a full-time job in the office of a local car dealership, and I worked part time at the Training School. We reckoned her forty hours at two and a nickel an hour and my twenty-ish hours at two and a half an hour would keep me in the classroom, food on the table, gas in the car, and clothes on our backs.

And that one-and-a-half-income strategy worked just fine.

For a while.

Dianne and I had been married only seven months when we learned that the two of us were about to become the three of us.

That would change things, and we knew it.

About the time her baby bump looked serious, Mom said adios to the work force. The rat race would have to get along with one less rat. That part didn't require much decision because we had no choice. What came next, though, required not only a decision but a commitment.

See, we realized we'd soon have to decide whether our

post-baby Mom would return to a job outside the home or commit to working full time in the home. With crummy pay.

This wasn't a simple choice by any stretch of the imagination. I mean, as a full-time student I could work only part-time hours, and nearly every life goal we had was centered on the completion of my schooling. So I wasn't *about* to drop out of school. My studenthood, or studency, or studentification—whatever you call it, it was nonnegotiable.

But whether we could continue to survive and meet our goals with only a single part-time income—well, that was the question of the day.

***

Married folk get to face a lot of tough decisions, no doubt about it. And in the post-honeymoon weeks and months, those decisions aren't only tough, they're new. For Dianne and me, there was a third dimension. Because we lived hundreds of miles away from parents—and nearly all other relatives, for that matter—and long-distance phone calls cost four legs and an arm or two, we found ourselves having to make those tough new decisions on our own, usually, with only each other to depend on for counsel, wisdom, sympathy, and support. If I said that it didn't feel like we carried the weight of the world on our backs, I'd be telling a great big story.

It did.

But in the rearview mirror, it all takes on a different shape and meaning.

Yep, blessings look funny sometimes.

In retrospect, I see that those times when we had to make hard decisions with only each other to rely on were the furnace in which a relationship was fired and finished. That was when we learned who we were and what we were capable of doing.

It was when we found a mutual trust and an interdependence that would stand the tests of time, overcome the challenges of life, and help us resolve the conflicts we would face together in years to come.

[*Failure-to-Launch Note:* What the tough times of our young life together fostered in our relationship seem to be the very things we parents sometimes unintentionally deny our married children when we give *too much* money, *too much* support, *too much* rescue. Yeah, it's not an easy thing to watch them struggle through difficult times, that's for dang sure. But what comes of *too much* help is ironically the very thing we shouldn't want for our children and their spouses: dependence on us instead of on each other.]

[*Failure-to-Launch Note PS:* It's not that our parents weren't there for us. They were. In fact, if you look up *supportive and loving parents* in the dictionary you'll find pictures of J. C., Mildred, Dale, and Joanne. No, Dianne and I were connected with our parents, and we knew it. It's just that they were wise enough to not impose themselves on us, and far enough away geographically that it wasn't convenient for us to turn to them whenever we hit a rough spot. But you can bet your last pfennig that they were there for us in those first years, and we knew that if ever we reached the end of our rope, we'd look up to see them at the other end, pulling like crazy. And they've been there for us every single day since.]

I'd have given a nickel for some of this rearview-mirror perspective when my sweetheart and I were in the middle of all those dang decisions and dilemmas. I mean, as principled or romantic or inspiring or brave as it all may sound now, facing harsh reality and figuring out how to solve our problems was just plain ol' gut-wrenching *hard*, when we were knee-deep in it all.

Somehow, though, Dianne and I managed that day to make a decision and a commitment that we thought right for us. Might not have been right for every husband-and-wife team in this whole big world, and probably wouldn't have been—but it seemed right for us.

We opted for a full-time, stay-at-home Mom after Baby came, with no idea how we'd stretch my meager income to make ends meet while we chased the goals that seemed bent on playing hide-and-seek with us.

***

Okay. Maybe I'm lying just a tad.

I mean, yeah . . . we adopted a stay-at-home-mom strategy and stuck to it, for the most part. But I admit—we veered once or twice. See, there were times when we decided that a short-term job for Mom while the children were young would allow us to reach some important goal. And when Mom did go to work, the children always remained our first priority.

Take buying our first house, for instance.

***

Truth be told, I don't know what I was thinking, that late-summer Saturday in '77. I was just lying comfortably there on that hand-me-down couch in our cozy—read: *tiny*—two-bedroom apartment. Pondering, perhaps, the perplexity of the Archer's Paradox. Wondering, maybe, whether the coming winter would provide sufficient snow for good ground cover and adequate spring water. Or considering, even, the possibility that Ogden and Ramsey may have inadvertently mistranslated Wittgenstein's *Tractatus Logico-Philosophicus*.

Nah. I was vegging out.

When it came, it hit me like a bolt of lightning, that

thought—and I arose from the couch, walked to the kitchen, hefted the telephone book from the small metal caddy beneath the wall phone, and said to Dianne as I thumbed the pages, "We need to buy a house."

Looking back, I understand her wide eyes and gaping mouth as my sweetheart stammered, "We . . . buy a . . . you said buy a what? Buy a house? A *house*?" I mean, we had about twenty cents in the ol' savings account, and our checking account was getting worked like a rented mule and spun like a two-dollar petty cash account. Even though I'd earned a bachelor's degree and was working as a psychologist, it was still uncommon—read: *unheard of*—for Morris household revenues and expenses to shake hands politely in any given month.

And yet there I was, casually tossing off the idea of buying a house like I had twenty-seven thousand smackaroos lying carelessly in the top drawer of my junkyard-surplus desk upstairs.

I didn't.

But that didn't stop me from opening that dang phone book and flipping to the "Realtors" section of the Yellow Pages. Never mind that it was Saturday and no one would be in the office. I perused the listed agencies and decided on one nearby, bookmarked the listed number with my index finger, lifted the wall phone's handset, and dialed the seven digits.

After a ring or two, I was pleasantly surprised to hear a real, live person say, "Neighborhood Realty. Can I help you?"

"Uh, yeah, I mean, I hope so. We'd like to buy a house."

I guess that must be a good thing for a realtor to hear. Anyway it seemed to be good news for this one. I presumed I was speaking to an agent, though she hadn't identified herself as such.

"Good," the friendly lady said. "That's very good. Maybe I can help you."

Then she explained how yes, she was an agent and no, she didn't usually come in on Saturday but there'd been some little something she'd forgotten to do or look at or take home with her yesterday. And there she was, where she usually wasn't on a Saturday.

By the end of our conversation, Ms. Realtor and I knew things about each other. She knew I wanted to buy a house. I knew she wanted to sell a house. She knew I didn't have a cent to my name. I knew she'd require money in return for a house. I knew she knew of a small housing development being planned on the other side of town—and that we could reserve a lot there, with no cash required from us till construction began in a few months.

Hmmm.

I wondered out loud whether that might give us time to save up a down payment.

"Precisely," our new best friend replied.

We signed a couple of good-faith-estimate papers, selected a basic bi-level floor plan of about nine hundred square feet, and devised a rough game plan that would take us across the threshold of our first house.

We hoped.

And then we went ahead and made the first move of that game, just like we knew what the heck we were doing.

Dianne took a job as a K-Mart cashier, working part-time evening and weekend shifts.

***

I've no idea whether it's true today or not, but in those days, our local K-Mart paid its employees in cash. The cash was distributed every Friday from an office at the back of the store. Now, if you put those two things together—paid in cash, at the back of the store—you may suspect a method to the madness. I mean, you pay people in cash after their shift ends and then make them tote those greenbacks through the clothing section and the electronics section and the records section and the household goods section . . . well, by the time your average employee got to the front of the store, he or she'd picked up enough stuff to assure the return of a sizable portion of that cash to the store and lovely vacations for K-Mart stockholders.

But we were saving for a house, dadgummit, and that was The Purpose of this job. We didn't need fancy clothes or a bigger TV or the new Barry Manilow LP or a magic potato peeler. Well, maybe we needed the new Manilow LP, but we didn't need the other stuff. And we simply couldn't afford that spend-every-cent-you-made-last-week-before-you-leave-the-store strategy.

I had a counter-strategy, and I implemented it without fail.

When I came home from work on Fridays, my first stop was at a neighboring apartment where my wife's brother Jim and his wife lived. Dianne's evening shift began shortly before I got home from work, so our sister-in-law, Nancy, was good enough to tend our sweet Anne till I arrived. It was her naptime, anyway—Anne's, not Nancy's—so the timing was just right. Just after naptime ended, I picked up Anne and headed for K-Mart. I parked my little green Datsun pickup truck in the parking lot that was roughly the size of Baltimore and walked, toddler in tow, into the store, where we kidnapped Mom and headed for the paymaster. She collected her cash-filled envelope from a rather stern-faced human resources critter and signed for it, then handed it to me—the envelope, not the stern-faced human resources critter. I stuffed the treasure into my pocket and transported it right on through the clothing section and the electronics section and the records section and the household goods section, out of the store and into the car. From there, it was a beeline to the bank, where I introduced those dollars—and every single quarter, dime, nickel, and penny—to the ones I'd previously deposited in our growing little pot that would be the down payment on our dream.

I did those things precisely—every single, solitary week.

And every time I made that deposit, I recalled the line from Frank Capra's "It's a Wonderful Life," spoken by James Stewart's George Bailey as he kissed and then almost prayerfully held up the last two remaining dollar bills of his honeymoon savings, the rest of which had just been used to stop a panicked run on Bailey's Building and Loan.

"A toast! A toast! A toast to Mama Dollar and to Papa Dollar, and . . . you better have a family real quick."[1]

***

Well, we stuck to our guns. Dianne worked herself nearly to death for the next few months, alternating between motherhood and cashiering—oh, and by the way, she was four months pregnant when she started this gig. Between my job and the master's program at the university, I stayed a bit busy myself—but I was able to lend a hand here and there. Together we managed to come up with a minimum down payment by the deadline and eventually moved into our beautiful—if compact—new home.

I say eventually because . . . well, because we hit a few snags along the way, as the house was being built. If you've enjoyed the—ahem—awesome experience of building a house, you're probably wondering out loud, right now: "What? Problems building a house? Can't imagine that . . ." I'm sure yours was built without a single challenge along the way. But, yeah, for us, there was a hitch or two. Like, for starters, waiting about twenty-seven years for construction to begin.

And when, finally, construction began, things just got worse.

***

Dianne and I drove by our empty lot every day at least once, to see whether there might be—oh, happy day!—some sign that a living human being had actually set foot on our property and *done* something. Heck, *anything* would've made us happy. Backhoe tracks. Survey lines. A dug-up weed lying limp on the ground. A dirt clod moved from one side of the lot to the other. Fresh tunnels suggesting that gophers were hightailing it to safer ground. Any little ol' difference would've been just great.

But, day after day after day—nothing.

And then, all at once—and I mean literally, from one day to the next . . . a swimming pool.

Confused? So were we when we drove by our lot, expecting to see the same ol' dirt lying around in the same ol' way—and instead found a big square hole full of water.

See, our lot was situated on lower ground than the adjacent lots. Low enough, in fact, that the construction plan called for the foundation of our little bi-level house to be built on the ground nearly as it lay, with only minor excavation. Then they'd haul in dirt to backfill and cover the foundation and basement, putting the house at ground level.

Apparently, the backhoe guy didn't get the memo about that *minor excavation* thing. He dug and he dug and he dug some more.

Mr. Backhoe, meet Mr. Water Table.

Yep, nature provided a lovely swimming pool where a foundation should've been.

About eighty-six years later—I'm rounding up—the pool finally got drained, and the menacing water was replaced by fill-dirt that was then compacted to the density of concrete. The foundation was poured, and wood and brick began to rise from it, slowly but . . .

I was gonna say *slowly but surely*, but it was *way* more slowly than surely.

In fact, I guess when the rough framing went up it looked really, really good to the builder 'cause he just flat didn't wanna do anything else to it. For the longest time.

So long a time, in fact, that we figured it just wasn't gonna happen without a little encouragement. Not that we hadn't tried to encourage Mr. Builder already. We had. But it was apparently gonna take someone with a bit more clout than we had to get this dude off the mark.

With a little research, we discovered the telephone number of the State Contractors Licensing Board—or whatever they called the agency that monitored building contractors and made them play nice—and placed a call. To the friendly man who answered the call I explained that we'd been waiting a year—yep, I said a *year*—for our little ol' nine-hundred-square-foot bungalow to begin its rise from the rubble. And now, I told him, the owner of our apartment would soon be changing our rental agreement to a lease agreement, and we had to get the heck outta Dodge before things got complicated. The nice man understood our plight and took our side. He thought we'd waited just about long enough. He asked for our contractor's name, I supplied it, and he politely dismissed me with the promise, "I'll take care of this."

He did.

Thirty minutes later, I was on the phone with our contractor.

"Mr. Morris, I just spoke with the Licensing Board," he told me, subdued. "I've been instructed to call you today and give you a completion date that I've gotta meet. We believe we can have your house ready for occupancy in two months from today."

Well, our experience with this whole thing up to that point didn't persuade us to much confidence. We believed he'd reach that goal, just about as much as we believed Tarzan's Tantor headed for the elephants' graveyard when he got sick.

Both seemed a bit mythical.

***

With an interesting mix of joy and trepidation, and even though the house wasn't yet completed, we signed the papers to finalize a thirty-year mortgage at a healthy interest rate of twelve percent. Yep, I said *twelve percent interest.* Now let me hear all the moans and wails out there about the current three-and-a-half percent rate.

[*Historical Inflation Note:* Because of prime lending and mortgage interest rates that soared out of control, many experts consider the years 1978 through the early 1980s to have been the worst time in the history of *ever* to build or buy a house.[2] The prime lending rate rose steadily and peaked at a record high of twenty-one-and-a-half percent on December 19, 1980, then remained in double digits until 1985.[3] When it came to buying a house, one might argue that Dianne and I had the timing of an auction bidder with a twitch. But I don't see it that way. To me, it was just another obstacle that we had to find a way around to meet an important goal.]

After signing on the dotted line, we followed construction

day to day. And we saw a house being built, that's true—but it became quickly and painfully clear that corners were being cut and mistakes made. I mean, you *could* walk on the pine-board staircase leading from the backyard up to the back door, but you'd better be feeling adventuresome because there was absolutely no guarantee that you'd reach the back door before the whole thing collapsed under your feet. And you could open the front door enough to squeeze through, but a misplaced wall inside prevented the door from opening fully, making it a tight squeeze for everyone except perhaps Olive Oyl.

Yes, we complained to the site foreman. No, it didn't do a whit of good.

Except that maybe it helped him make the very good decision to quit his job. Or else someone made the decision for him. I don't know. In any case, he disappeared—and I can only hope the poor guy found a new line of work. And happiness in it.

Of course the new foreman got our house completely finished and ready for us to move into, without problem or delay.

Not.

Well, he got it to the point of being *occupiable*—sort of.

Apparently our contractor was right friendly with inspectors and other code-enforcers or else somebody owed somebody something or somebody had something on somebody or . . . well, or *something.* Whatever the explanation, everyone seemed willing to turn his little head and look the other way for a moment while we moved into our house on the date promised, even though the front door still wouldn't open all the way and the first step out the back door was a doozie—as in, fifteen feet straight down to a splatter on hard, bare ground. See, the flimsy back door staircase and deck had been torn down but not yet replaced.

So the bad news was that we couldn't use the back door and had to make darn sure our little ones didn't venture too close to it. The good news was that we were in our house, at long last—and we lived payment-free for more than three months while all the details were being finished.

Mr. Builder suffered a fatal heart attack shortly after our subdivision was put in order. I'd wonder out loud what caused that myocardial infarction, but I'd rather not belabor the obvious.

***

Just yesterday I was comparing notes with Dianne to make sure the chronology of this story was accurate.

I try very hard not to lie.

The discussion took us on a brief but lovely walk down memory lane, which we enjoyed. But while we enjoyed the jaunt, we found it difficult to realize that we actually made it through all the stuff we made it through. Looking back, we can nail down the details of *what* we did, but the *how* of it . . . well, that's a different kettle of fish.

It's hard to remember just *how* we were able to do everything that we had to do in order to finally occupy the house we'd dreamed of. I mean, we both worked in and out of the home, day and night. To make sure one of us was nearly always with our children, we lived schedules so complicated they made the Internal Revenue Code look like a second-grader's first essay. We faced a deadline for saving a down payment while hanging from a budget that was always *anything* but balanced. We had the pressures of our jobs and the stress of my graduate school classes. We fought gruesome Gettysburg battles with our builder and blinked back the disappointment of delayed goals. And in the middle of it all, we welcomed our second child, Kristopher, to the chaos.

None of this singles us out for medals, I know that. Others have survived such things, and more. But it seems nevertheless a worthy accomplishment, and I'm glad I can say we did it.

We is the operative word. Without a willingness to share the responsibilities and the work and the stresses—although I'll grant that my sweet Dianne shouldered the lion's share—perhaps we may never have come out, intact, on the other side.

Here's where I give a respectful tip of the cap and a hearty "way-to-go" to all those parents who've done all this and more without a partner to share the work and the stress and the burden.

And the joy.

I empathize with those unsung heroes, but I'm glad I had someone to share the difficult times with, and I'm pleased with what the two of us became as we trudged through mistakes, setbacks, and all. It was hard, every single piece of it—harder than anything we'd done before. But as fulfilling as anything we've done since.

It was truly the furnace in which a worthy relationship was fired and finished.

And I'd do it all over again, if I could do it with my children's mother.

NOTES

1. *It's a Wonderful Life*, directed by Frank Capra (Hollywood: Liberty Films [II], 1946).

2. Council for Economic Education, "The Early 1980s: A Tough Time for Home Builders and Mortgage Bankers," accessed June 28, 2012, http://www.econedlink.org/lessons/index.php.

3. No author, "Prime Interest Rate History: History of the U.S. (Fed) Prime Interest Rate from 1957 to the Present," accessed June 28, 2012, http://www.fedprimerate.us/wall_street_journal_prime_rate_history.htm.

FOUR

PONYTAILS AND LUNCH MONEY

Not everything that's required of a daddy is icky.

Oh, in the first couple of years of Baby's life, it's kinda hard to duck The Disgusting Duty that seems always at hand. That's true enough. But as the little rugrats grow bigger and older, the things they require of a dad become less and less gross but more and more challenging.

Yep, the job of being a daddy just gets "curiouser and curiouser," as Miss Alice was wont to say.[1] Whether he's beating back the monsters of the workaday world to earn enough scratch to put and keep a roof over his family, or from time to time overcoming inherent male weaknesses to make his daughters pretty in ponytails and his sons handsome in hand-me-downs, Daddy's contributions to the family can be varied and invaluable.

Plus he's enjoying moments that'll be the stuff and fabric of at least two things, if he pays attention.

***

During the weeks and months of Dianne's save-for-our-down-payment employment, guess who had the responsibility for child-care duties. Oh, we occasionally used the services of a friendly babysitter, but rarely; by and large, Daddy was in charge of the household whenever Mom was scuffling around K-Mart, helping people find what they couldn't do without.

In fact, the main reason Mom elected to work evening and weekend shifts was that I was available for Anne during those times and we wouldn't have to use a babysitter.

For most of this K-Mart gig, our little girl was potty-trained, so I had little to worry about in that regard—and that wasn't really such a problem for me, anyway, as I've already pointed out. And as for baby food . . . well, I didn't have to suppress the ol' gag reflex quite so often as the little tyke grew older and felt more like using her little fingers and gnawing on stuff.

But one duty never went away and, in fact, got more complicated by the day.

Grooming.

Now, even as a young father I knew about *some* things. Heck, I was a college graduate, after all, and working a professional job. I knew about the id and the ego, and about Pavlov's dogs and metronome. I knew about operant conditioning, and I knew that behavior modification worked great on other people's kids. I knew other stuff too, about movies, music, sports, poetry. Heck, I could even tie a halfway decent half-hitch, if its quality was negotiable.

But what I knew about grooming little girls you could write on the head of a pin. And given a choice about it, I'd have just as soon passed on the whole deal.

Sometimes I didn't have that choice. I mean, sometimes I had to take my girl out into the big bad world without Mommy around to help, and it just wouldn't do to have the little nipper look like she'd been holed up with an ornery she-panther in a high mountain cave for the winter.

I'm lying just a tad when I say I wasn't good with grooming. Some tasks were no problem. I was OK with putting on a diaper and protective outer panties. I could snap on a onesie just as slick as you please. I could wash a face, brush a tooth, tie a shoe, clip a nail with the best of 'em.

But hair. Now, that was a different story. A sadder story.

Most of the time, after I'd combed Anne's hair, she looked like she'd stood in front of a wind machine for a week or two. Or like she'd just pulled her finger from an electrical socket.

It wasn't a pretty sight. The hair, I mean. The girl, otherwise, was gorgeous.

And don't think she didn't know it when I'd goofed up the hair. She did. When her mom dressed and groomed her, our sweet daughter looked like she was headed for a child fashion magazine shoot, and she knew the difference between that look and the one I inflicted on her.

Kinda like our family pet, Gavan, after a visit to the groomer back in '65.

***

Shortly after we moved to California in '63, a close friend of the family gave us a white adult poodle named Gavan. Actually, she first gave us an adult white-and-apricot parti poodle named Coquette, but the little critter was so traumatized by our family, I guess, that she had some kind of a nervous breakdown. Mercifully, we returned her. Gavan was the replacement, and he was weird, so he liked our family just fine.

A lot of the time Gavan looked like he'd just rolled down a hill, but occasionally we treated him to a nice grooming at the local pet store. Shampoo and blow-dry. Stylish clipping, with fluffy shoulders and topknot, pillowed ears, bare midriff, puff-ball on the tip of his tail. A red ribbon here and there. Shiny nails. Perfumed talc. The works.

Returning home after his very first grooming, Gavan was all about prancing through the house, showing off his fresh new look to anyone who'd take notice. And when someone took notice, the little guy was proud as a peacock. Threw his head back, stuck that tail into the air, and strutted like Streisand on the Academy Awards red carpet. And he smiled. *Smiled*, I tell you. He loved the attention. Oh, yeah. Loved it.

But Gavan just had to have Tiki's approval in this thing, I guess. Tiki was my black-and-white tomcat roughly the size of Ireland, and a no-nonsense kind of critter. If animals worked jobs, this cat would've been more likely found in an oil field than at a university. And although he tolerated Gavan's annoying crush, he'd have been happy to have the doggone dog gone.

Quick as that, the primped poodle had tracked his feline friend and was sashaying back and forth and forth and back, trying like the dickens to impress the whatsit out of him. Now, Tiki just couldn't care less about all this froufrou and stinkum. He walked up to his spruced-up roommate, took a leisurely lap or two around him while eyeballing him up one side and down the other, had a little sniff here and there, and then threw his head into the air as if to say, "*Peeeeeuw,* Dog!" Then he walked away.

In that moment of rejection, Gavan's countenance dropped with a thud so nearly literal you'd swear you heard it. His head drooped, his tail fell, and he crouched and slithered away in shame, shrinking from the world. Under the TV he crawled, and that's where he stayed for the next week.

Okay, so Anne was no poodle, and I don't mean to draw that likeness. But when her mother spiffed her up all nice and pretty, this toddler knew she could hold her own in the presence of any Shirley Temple–type that might show up. When Daddy took a brush to that beautiful hair and turned it into something else, she knew the difference.

If she'd thought about it, I suppose she might've crawled under the TV when she saw me and that brush headed her way.

I had to do something to fix this problem.

***

It was simply a matter of focus and commitment, you know, no more or less than what's required to graduate college or buy a house or do any other worthwhile thing. I just had to make up my mind that I'd figure out a better way to do this hair thing, and practice till I could do it right.

Turns out it was all about teamwork between the right and left hands. With my right, I brought the brush up the underside of Anne's hair, toward me. The brush wasn't broad enough to capture all the hair, but it corralled most of it, and my left hand took care of the overflow. After brushing upward once and using my left hand to contain all the hair, I could then brush any way I wanted. Underside or topside strokes, it made no difference. And I could do either kind of stroke as many times as I wanted or needed to, to shape the hair in my left hand just so.

I'm headed toward a ponytail here.

Once I got the hair brushed and shaped just so in my left hand, I could drop the brush and pick up an elastic hair band—the finishing touch for the do. At first it was tough enough just to get that hair pulled through the band without creating a snarl that required garden shears. But even harder was keeping the ponytail centered while I applied the band. *That*, my friend, took some practice. And many times I finished the job only to look down and realize that the dang ponytail wasn't in the back, where it was supposed to be, but sticking out the side of Anne's head, where it wasn't supposed to be. I learned to adjust it, and before long the little puppy was centered right square at the back of that pretty little head.

Eventually I could do a ponytail on each side. Maybe you call those pigtails. I don't know. But I do know it was hard to center both of them properly. Worth the trouble, though, 'cause when I hit the target, my baby looked just as cute as cute. And it added a little variety. Pretty darn upscale for a dad, if you ask me.

And the ponytail always told a tale: whenever our sweet Anne was sporting one—or two, as the case may have been—everyone knew Daddy had been on the job.

***

You know, you've just gotta pity the first child. Heck, that poor little varmint catches it all. I mean, here you've got these brand-new parents trying to figure everything out as they go. How to feed a baby, bathe a baby, dress a baby, soothe a baby . . . well, just almost *everything* to do with a baby is new to these first-timers. And that first kid's gotta endure all the practice, all the mistakes, all the . . . well, just the whole parent break-in period, that's what the first kid out of the chute gets to endure.

When I think back on all the first-time-dad weirdness I inflicted on my little Anne, I'm surprised she still comes over to the house for dinner on Sundays.

Lest you think I played favorites, rest assured that Kristopher and Jeremy didn't fare much better than Anne did when they were in Dad's clutches. Oh, I tried to improve from one kid to the next, and maybe I did this thing or that a little better than I'd done it last time—but each of the boys was obliged to pay those dues, just like his older sister did.

Of course, little girls and little boys are quite different in many ways. And while that may be stating the incredibly obvious, I've run into those who believe the only differences between a little boy and a little girl are those we teach them.

I don't think so.

In fact, I'll be so bold as to propose that anyone who doesn't believe little boys and little girls come into this world hardwired differently simply never raised a little boy and a little girl.

Whether you'll give on that point or not, perhaps you'll agree that child-care duties vary a bit on account of gender. Anyway, I found it to be so.

For example, I found dressing and grooming my boys to be less challenging than dressing and grooming my daughter. My boys didn't have enough hair to worry about, so sprucing them up was kinda like the *Reader's Digest* version of hair care. Gimme a spray of water and a comb, and we were good to go. And I didn't need the world's greatest fashion sense to dress the little guys, because in those days you had about as much choice in boys' clothing and fashion as you had in paying taxes: None, in either. Little girls' fashion was to die for, but I guess nobody who sewed for a living gave a darn about little boys.

Today, fashion options for the xy-chromosome-type kidlets are way different. Heck, you can find Nike shoes for little boys that look just like Dad's or better, Levi's jeans that are custom cut for little critters and better looking than Hawaii off the port bow, polo shirts that Dad could wear if he lost a pound or two. Yeah, you've got *choices* in toddler boys' fashions—now.

Oh, I suppose we had choices when my boys were little—but they were limited. You could buy white shoes or black shoes. You could buy ugly pants or uglier pants. You could buy a plain shirt or a plain shirt that didn't fit.

It got a little better as everybody got older, though. Well, I say *better*, and as far as fashion choice, it's true. But it's also true that in other ways, things got a bit more complex.

Take that name-brands-versus-K-Mart battle that seems destined to be fought with every new generation. You know what I'm talking about. It's when it's suddenly all about that patch on the pants pocket or that emblem on the shirt or that air pump in the sneakers. Seems like there was always some brand that the kids just wouldn't dare be seen in public without.

At about a bazillion times the cost.

Of course, it was a good time to teach some important lessons about values and frugality and breaking-away-from-the-masses. You know, a time when you could say to the kids, "So if your friends all jumped off the cliff, would you follow?"

We parents never miss an opportunity to overwork a cliché.

But every time I felt an urge to chastise or correct or teach a lesson about how ridiculous this name-brand thing was . . . well, that's when I flashed back to my high school days and saw in my mind's eye the Levi's 501s and London Fog jackets and Corbin trousers and brass belt buckles and Florsheim wing tips and Keds deck shoes that always managed to find a way onto my worthless body, when something with a Sears label would've covered me just as well.

For a lot less.

There's nothing new under the sun.

And this name-brands battle was only one of the ways in which life with growing children got more complex. But, in the main, this well-meaning dad tended to be a bit oblivious to such adolescence nuances. Not that I didn't wanna know about everything my kids were doing while I was out capturing the bacon and filling my head with graduate school stuff. And it's not to say that I didn't make it to tennis matches and basketball games and concerts. I did. Nothing could keep me away from that stuff. But as for day-to-day routines that had to be monitored and taken care of by some responsible adult-type parent with patience and money and a car . . .

Mom had it all covered.

***

When all three kids were in school for a full day, Mom gave some thought to trying the job market again, on a limited basis. In our community lived a couple of high-rankers in an up-and-coming local software company, and one of them asked Dianne if she'd consider a receptionist job at the main office. She was interested but, as always, sensitive to the needs of the children. Color us surprised when the company's vice president agreed to a schedule that allowed her to come into the office after our children left for school, and be home in time to greet the little rascals at the door when they came home.

She accepted the job and became one of the first one hundred thirty or so employees of a small but rapidly growing company that would eventually boast thousands of employees.

The receptionist job description was short lived. Before you could whistle a chorus of "Leaving on a Jet Plane," Dianne was in the marketing end of things, coordinating trade shows and events—primarily in Canada, at first, but after the company was acquired by another, she found herself in New York, San Francisco, Paris, Tokyo, Munich, and who-knows-where.

So the Morris family eventually found itself minus a mom for roughly one week out of every month. During the other weeks, she was a nine-to-fiver, but for that one week, Mom jetted there and then here, doing her job in the only way she's ever known how to do anything.

With excellence.

***

Perhaps we don't pay close enough attention to the importance of *timing* in life. It's an incredibly important matter. I mean, what we're capable of thinking or doing or enduring or appreciating when we're young isn't necessarily what we're capable of thinking or doing or enduring or appreciating when we're a bit long in the tooth.

With years and experience, it seems our capacities expand.

I mean, if I'd found myself with such household responsibilities a dozen years or so before Dianne started globetrotting, I'd have been a case. I mean, a *case*.

But when the time came, I was up to the task. I wasn't pursuing any degrees, and I was working a job that gave me the flexibility to play both Dad and Mom for a few days each month.

Timing's everything.

And when I say I was *up to the task*, I might be rounding up some. See, at first I found it a bit annoying that I had to balance my working-world-father duties with homemaking duties. Yeah, things were no longer quite as simple for me as an occasional pin under the thumbnail or gagging on baby food or fixing a ponytail. Now there were meals and schedules and lunch money and basketball practice and school projects and church meetings and groceries and piano lessons and concerts and field trips and dirty clothes to occupy my what-used-to-be-free time. Life was suddenly more complicated, and I felt a bit picked on. And I can't say—although I wish like heck I could—that I was calm and collected and patient and poised every single minute of every single day.

I wasn't, but I tried.

What I can say is that I developed some serious appreciation for the details of my children's lives. And from where I stand at this moment, I'd support a law that *requires* moms to be out of the house for a few days every once in a while, just so dads could know all the things their loving, nurturing, patient, service-inclined, organized, capable partners do every day of their lives while children are in the nest.

They'd enjoy, too, some amazing payback.

See, one thing I learned from doing the daddy thing is that, done properly, it's a two-way street. A win-win deal, so to speak. The kids get to know Dad and maybe even pick up a worthwhile thing or two from him along the way. In return, Dad gets to know his young'uns better and be reminded of what makes a kid tick. He knew it once upon a time, because he was one himself—but years too often put the wrong kind of space between dads and their memories.

But all it takes to get it back, I guess, is a job that sends Mom out of town for a week every now and again. As he covers the home front, Dad gets to learn about lunch money and piano lessons and school projects and whatnot, and he gets to learn just how important a dad can be to the nurturing—not just the feeding and clothing—of the children.

Don't jump to a wrong conclusion. There was no family desertion here. Mom's job grew more complex only as the children aged and grew more independent. They learned well the lessons their mother taught them, and each of them gracefully and timely shed a youthful chrysalis to reveal a terrific, well-balanced, caring, responsible young woman or man.

If they hadn't been my children, I'd have wanted them for friends.

***

If the things Daddy contributes to the cause during infant and toddler years are the building blocks of bonding between father and child, the things he can contribute during childhood and adolescent years are the cement that unifies those blocks and transforms them into a solid foundation of mutual love, understanding, and respect.

And through it all he's racking up moments that'll be the stuff and fabric of at least two things, if he pays attention:

A relationship with his children that endures and fosters a happiness in family and a joy in posterity that only a committed, available, involved father can know.

And memories that'll warm and comfort and enliven him later, providing shelter against the ravages of what otherwise would be the colder, bleaker days of a life passing way too swiftly.

NOTES

1. Lewis Carroll, *Alice's Adventures in Wonderland* (New York: Barnes & Noble, Inc., 2010), 23.

FIVE

LITTLE SURPRISES AND CLOSE CALLS

From the time they cry their way into this unsuspecting world till they get chucked from the nest, with kids it's just one thing after another. If I had a dollar—no, I'd only need a nickel—for every time I got a surprise or a shock or a scare or a smile from my little ones through the years, I'd have millions.

Heck, I might even be rich enough to fill my car's gas tank.

Yeah, wherever you find a kid you're gonna find excitement, no doubt about it.

And it's a good thing too. Otherwise we parents might never have occasion to use all those nifty clichéd instructions and warnings and ultimatums we seem to love so much.

You're gonna put an eye out. I hope you brought enough for everyone. I'm not gonna tell you again. Just wait till your father gets home. I'm gonna turn this car around. You should've gone before we left. I'll give you something to cry about. It'll never heal if you pick at it. Keep your hands to yourself. Not another word, mister. Your face is gonna freeze like that. Someday you'll thank us for this.

So many standard-equipment phrases available to parents, not even counting the ones I'm sorry I ever used. You probably know the ones I'm talking about.

The thing about kids is, they never really let you get your feet under you between adventures. In fact, there *isn't* any *between* adventures. Not really. It's like the adventure begins as soon as the first little rascal moves around the house under its own power and ends when the last little rascal moves out of the house under its own power. Yep, it's all just one long, continuous, amazing, difficult, happy, frustrating, exciting adventure.

And I wouldn't take a million dollars for any single minute of it.

***

Seems like every parent looks forward to seeing that first baby get around all by itself. I mean, heck . . . just thinking about giving those overworked baby-lugging arm muscles a rest and imagining all the arm space that'll be freed up to tote stuff here and there . . . well, it's enough to make you covet that movement. That ambulation. That independence.

Just shows how dumb parents can be.

Before you can say *Sit down, mister, and don't even twitch*, we discover that with this coveted movement and ambulation and independence come supervision issues we'd never imagined. Yeah, it all starts innocently enough with that rolling over—*awwww*, isn't that *cute*!—but before you can hum a chorus of "Walk on the Wild Side," that kid's belly-crawling and then creeping and then rising to its feet and then right away getting in a hurry. There's just no slowing down after that—and the whole durn world changes, forever.

Now don't judge me on this, but I sometimes question the sequence of human development. I certainly don't wanna take issue with the Creator on this thing, but my finite mortal brain wonders about the wisdom in letting a little human critter learn how to move all over the place by itself before it can reason about whether *over there's* a good place to go or not.

Seems kinda glitchy, if you ask me.

One thing's for dang sure, though: that gap between Baby-can-move and Baby-can-reason makes Mom and Dad pay pretty darn good attention and persuades them to become keenly aware of every staircase, every electrical outlet, and every breakable whatchamacallit under the roof.

***

When our little Anne first started getting from here to there on all fours and then on unsure legs, we were living in a split-level apartment. You entered on ground level and then went downstairs to the living room and kitchen, or upstairs to the bedrooms and bath. Stairs aren't what most parents would consider to be *good* things where there's a kidlet cleaning the carpet with its hands and knees or stumbling here and falling there—and the thought of what might happen on or around those stairs in an unguarded moment keeps Mom and Dad on constant alert and the medicine cabinet stocked with Bromo Seltzer. Or Alka Seltzer, if you prefer.

Maybe it's a girl-guy thing, I don't know. But it seems true that moms are usually a bit more cautious and worrisome about such things than dads are. Not that dads don't worry *at all*—just not as much as moms. I think. On average. Probably. Maybe. Or not.

It's multiple-choice PC.

Whether any difference in worry is a variable of gender or not, it's true that Dianne was more sensitive about those stairs than I was.

To tell the truth, I worried more about the danger of her worrying about the danger than I worried about the danger she worried about.

Whew.

We took precautions, of course. We had those crummy little accordion-gates that you wedged however you could wedge them at the top and/or bottom of the stairs, and that gave a bit of comfort. Still, it was clear that a child could dislodge the thing by leaning against it just right—and if a leaning child dislodged it, bad things were sure to happen immediately after.

As a psychologist, I picked up a few things about shaping behavior. The kids I worked with had severe or profound learning disabilities, so I was obliged to use basic, simple techniques to teach them life skills. It usually started with an analysis of whatever task was to be taught. For example, if I wanted Hector to learn to put on his coat, I'd break that big task into a bunch of little tasks, all of which had to be learned, in sequence, in order for him to put that coat on.

Sometimes we taught the steps in reverse order. It's called backward chaining: The last step of the sequence was taught first and the first step last. The idea was that after he mastered the first step in the sequence, the little guy could don a coat all by himself.

Frankly, I didn't care much for that backward chaining trumpery. Didn't work well for me.

But that task analysis stuff—now, *that* worked.

So I figured . . . well, worked there, oughta work here.

I took my little rugrat right over to the stairs and started teaching her, a piece at a time, to conquer a stair and then back down. Then two stairs. Then a few stairs. It took surprisingly little time to teach my baby to manage all the big bad stairs. Before you could say, *Halfway down the stairs is a stair where I sit*, she was handling that staircase with the skill and confidence of Tarzan shinnying up a Musanga cecropioides.

Now we didn't have to worry quite so much about disasters on those scary old stairs, although we continued to be cautious.

I'm glad I taught Anne to manage those stairs instead of avoiding them, because something occurred to me as I taught. As I see it, there's an inherent wisdom in teaching a child how to behave safely in the face of unavoidable hazard. See, there are just all kinds of obstacles and dangers and risks—*stairs*, if you will—that a child's gotta face while growing into a person. And if a parent's only strategy is to structure the child's world to *avoid* those stairs . . . well, that's just asking for trouble. And sure as drunk skunks can't skate straight, that trouble's gonna raise its ugly head, sooner or later. I mean, yeah . . . everything's just ducky, as long as guardrails are up and Mom or Dad's nearby to make sure the unthinkable doesn't happen. Trouble is, there will always be times when the rails are down or Mom and Dad can't be near enough.

We decided to make it a point through the years to teach our daughter to face and manage all kinds of stairs, instead of fearing and avoiding them.

For thirty-seven years, she's handled stairs just fine.

***

As if it weren't enough that kidlets face dangers inside the house, there's all that space outside that offers so much opportunity for a parent to rue that first step.

And sometimes machinery's involved.

I don't know who decided that two wheels are better than three to get kids from here to there, but maybe he was wrong. Ever think of that? Maybe three wheels is a better idea than two, even for older kids. And we could change this tradition if we wanted. I mean, if dads everywhere joined hands, sang a chorus or two of Kumbaya, and agreed that the three-wheeler would forever replace the two-wheeler as children's primary transportation . . . well, there'd just be a lot fewer daddies in the world with torn pants and broken bodies.

But in keeping with social custom, the Morris kids graduated from three wheels to two when it was time.

And guess who got to teach them how to ride the bloodthirsty, daddy-eating, two-wheeled monstrosities.

Well, I'm lying just a bit. No one taught Anne.

See, we gave our oldest her first bike when she was six or so, but it just leaned against the side of the house, unused. Little Anne just didn't seem to care about this biking thing. Before we knew it, days had turned to weeks, and weeks to months, and the new sky-blue bike with faux Stingray handlebars, banana seat, and flowered basket still stood parked under the carport.

And now Kristopher, our second, was interested in having a bike too.

No sense buying another bike right now, I thought. Heck, there was a brand-new two-wheeler outside, just yearning to be useful. Yeah, it was a girl's bike, but I figured a five-year-old boy wouldn't be too concerned about that little detail.

He wasn't.

So I broke out the shiny new bike and geared up to give my first bike-riding lessons.

Man your stations.

***

Now, to teach a child to ride a bike, some dads installed training wheels—but I couldn't see any point to that. Heck, as far as I could tell, all that came of such cheating was bent training wheels and a lopsided bike that moved about as fast as a snail on his way to a dentist appointment. And when the bent and broken and worn-out contraption eventually came off the bike's back wheel, the biker still couldn't ride a two-wheeler and was back to square one.

No training wheels for us. We just went for it, the old-fashioned way.

Seemed like a fairly simple thing, anyhow. Put the boy on the bike, push the two of them down the road, tell him to pedal, and voila! A cyclist he would be.

The putting-the-boy-on-the-bike part worked out just fine. I held the bike by the seat and the handlebars to stabilize it while he climbed aboard.

No problem.

To prepare him for what would come next I told him to put a foot on each pedal.

No problem.

I told him I was gonna run alongside and support him till we got up a little speed.

No problem.

Finally, I told him to keep pedaling after I let go, and just head for the north forty.

Problem.

My plan, of course, was to stay in the picture till it was clear that my son had things under control—then slow down, back off, and let him go on under his own power.

And to brag just a mite, everything was going both hunky

and dory, first time out of the chute. I was running alongside for support. Kristopher had the bike under control and was pedaling to beat the band. I let go and reminded him to keep pedaling. He did.

Easy peasy lemon squeezy.

But as I slowed my pace a bit and began to drop back, Kristopher noticed and realized I wasn't helping him stay up.

Now, one might think it would be good news for the rider, knowing that he's under his own power. But for a little boy on a bike for the first time, I guess it isn't such good news. It's more in the line of oh-my-holy-heck-now-I'm-gonna-get-creamed news.

Suddenly confused, Kristopher turned his head toward me, and his body followed. The bike took its lead from the body and listed to port. I saw right off where this sequence was taking us, but it was out of my hands. I could only hope that whatever friendly spirits are charged with protecting little boys and dads at moments such as this were paying close attention.

When I saw the bike and rider falling, I charged forward, hoping to get my hands back on the frame in time to steady it and stop the crash. But they were already past the point of no return, that bike and rider—and in a heartbeat, I knew there was nothing to be done but finish this fall and hope for as good an ending as possible.

Well, it was a horrendous crash.

The bike . . . I mean, I . . . I mean, we . . .

I took a technical writing class in college. I was assigned to select some object and make a written description of it with enough detail and precision that a reader who'd never seen the object could draw it or build it.

I decided on a fishhook. You'd think I'd have thought to choose a book or a tire or something big enough that I could use broad strokes to describe it. But heck no. I chose a dang fishhook, with its tiny loop at the top, barbed point, curves, and micro barbs along the shaft.

If you think it wasn't a difficult assignment, perhaps you'd like to give it a go.

When I tried, four paragraphs ago, to describe that horrendous crash with the detail to help you visualize it, I was reminded of how hard it was to describe the dang barbs on that fishhook.

I struggled through the horrors of depicting that tackle back in '73 only because it was an assignment. But this isn't an assignment, so you're gonna have to use your imagination to envision how awful that crash was because it's just too hard to properly describe the horror.

Here are some bullets, though, to help you out a bit.

Elbows, kneecaps, bike, falling, boy, yelling, dad, somersaults, sidewalk, asphalt, road rash, rips, bruises, dadgummit, bleeding, ouch.

Don't worry. Kristopher was unscathed. The bike was unbent.

Dad was half dead.

For about a week after that, I walked like Amos McCoy with a leg cramp.

Now, if you google "teaching a child to ride a bike," you'll find some nice, sensible, logical, sound steps to follow. But beware. You may also find a suggestion that you should always teach bike riding on a flat, hard, paved surface like a road or parking lot or sidewalk.

You're just as welcome as Barstow rain to follow that suggestion if you like. But I guaran-dang-TEE you'll never catch me and any child or grandchild of mine taking a maiden bike voyage on pavement or concrete or hard surface of any kind.

Never again.

And if the task of teaching a youngster to ride a bike lurks menacingly in your future, I suggest you consider rolling that little critter on something a smidgen friendlier than pavement.

Anyway, that's what I did.

Yep, from the day of The Horrendous Crash, it was ever after the soft, well-mown grass of the nearby elementary school for us.

***

I said no one taught Anne to ride a bike. Perhaps you wonder how she learned.

After I glued my broken body back together, I pointed out to my little girl that if her brother learned to ride that little blue bike before she did, then perhaps it oughta be his. I was kidding, but only partly. No reason to let a brand-new two-wheeler languish under the carport, unused.

"But that's *my* bike!" she protested.

"Well, sweetie, that's true. But you're not riding it or even trying to learn."

With a look on her face that was an odd mix of pouty and angry and I'll-show-you, Anne stood, walked out the back door and down the outside stairs, rolled the bike from the wall, sat on the banana seat, and rode away.

Don't ask me. I don't know.

***

Sometimes children can muster up mischievous moments that are downright scary.

Perhaps you've been in a department store with a child in tow and dropped the little guy's hand for just a moment so you could slide the shirts or blouses around the rack, searching for *that* style in *that* size. Perhaps you've then reached to take that little paw again, only to find that both the paw and the kidlet it was attached to were gone. Just like that.

You probably ran around the rack like a crazed person and then to the main aisle to see if he'd wandered a few steps away. Sighting nothing encouraging in the aisle, the next tactic was calling quietly and then loudly for him—and still seeing nothing, rushing to the nearest register to ask a clerk to make a quick overhead announcement while you continued your frantic search.

And oh! the horrible thoughts of unimaginable possibilities that flittered across your mind.

Panic city.

And all this right before the little guy poked his head out through the shirts hanging from a nearby round aluminum rack, grinning like a Scot with a secret.

Count the gray hairs on a parent's noggin and you'll know the number of such scares.

Jeremy did that very thing at a department store when he was a little fellow, and it scared the whatsit out of his mother and me. But he upped the ante one day at the Colorado River.

***

When the children were small, we went on car safari from time to time. Usually those vacations centered on visits to grandparents and aunts and uncles. Dianne's folks lived in Southern California, so visiting them required little travel time and not all that much gas money. A visit to the Mississippi Morrises was a bit more complex. Airfare for the lot of us cost more than our budget could take, so we also made that two-thousand-mile trip in a motor vehicle. Even though car travel taxed our bank account less than airfare for five, the cost and travel time still made it impractical to enjoy the southern journey as often as we'd have liked.

A silver Ford Granada Ghia took us to the Deep South the first time, as a full family of five. No air-conditioning, mind you, and that made things interesting. Riding in a sedan with three small children and no cooler was tough enough in the dry western and Midwestern air, but when we hit that wall of southern humidity somewhere near Missouri . . . well, that was something else again. I mean, it was like Mother Nature hauled off and hit you in the face with a wet steamy brick. All of a sudden somebody was hanging from every open window and panting like Fido.

The second trip to Mississippi was more comfortable. We'd bought a custom-built Toyota truck-and-camper rig from Dianne's parents, and the extra space for the kids was a heaven-send.

And both cab and camper were air-conditioned.

[*Travel Safety Note:* At the time, camper travel safety wasn't much of an issue. To us, it seemed simply a comfortable way to travel with children. Thirty years later, there's considerable discussion between opposing sides about whether passengers should be allowed in moving campers. Heck, I don't know. Pick whichever side you like and be ready to argue, I suppose.]

Every minute of travel in the Ford had been sheer torture, so we'd made our first trip to Dixie as fast as that six-cylinder would take us, stopping only now and again to grab a quick burger or for somebody to make a mad dash into a service station restroom. But we were comfortable traveling in the truck, so we stretched the second trip out a bit, stopping here and there to enjoy this or that monument or ghost town or world's largest ball of tinfoil or scenery.

Like the Colorado River, for example.

***

It was easily accessed, that lookout point at Lee's Ferry. After crossing the bridge over the Colorado River, we had only to veer from the highway onto an unpaved lot and park the truck. From there, it was just a good stretch of the legs to an area from which one could enjoy the majesty and splendor of the river flowing many hundreds of feet below.

I was having fun using a video camera we'd borrowed from a generous brother. It was 1985, and video technology was still in its infancy—so the recording unit I used was in two pieces: a handheld camera attached by cable to a recording unit slung over my shoulder.

A far cry from today's technology where every metal thing you have can take pictures.

We passed through the remains of old adobe brick buildings and made our way single-file down a dusty, rocky hill to a viewing area where a stone wall stood about thirty inches high or so. On the other side of that wall was a drop of about, oh, say twenty-seven bazillitrillion miles, straight down to the mighty Colorado winding its way through the canyon.

And I mean *just* on the other side of that wall.

Now, you need to understand my relationship with heights. It's not good. I guess I'd rather be chained to the floor of a moth hatchery in wool underwear than be any higher than my tippy-toes will take me. Air the least bit thinner than that sends my brain into some kind of gyration that's so awful I have to spell *dizzy* with three Zs.

So I hated that wall. Big, nasty, *mean* hated it. Well, I didn't hate the *wall* per se—only what was on the other side of it. Left to myself, I wouldn't have gotten within a mile of the dang thing. Couldn't disappoint the kids, though, so I screwed my courage to the sticking-place, gritted my pearly whites, and dragged my fear-stiffened body a slow step at a time to the edge of the wall. Looked over it and down—through the camera as I recorded.

Oh . . . my . . . holy . . . *heck*. It was *w-a-a-a-a-y* far to that river below, and it felt like nothing stood between me and that drop except the good sense not to be there.

But there I was. To tell the cowardly truth, if nobody'd been watching, I'd have turned and run back up the hill, screaming and waving my hands in the air like a converted heathen at a Billy Sunday revival.

That's what I *wanted* to do, but I didn't do it.

A daddy's gotta be brave, you know.

Now, on the way down that hill, we'd let our little nature lovers stretch their legs a bit, but they hadn't wandered far and were always in sight. As we stood in front of the wall, gawking at some of the Creator's finest handiwork, they were all within an arm's reach of Mom or Dad.

Thank heaven.

Well, if the incredible panorama of this canyon and snaking river didn't deserve a little videotape, I don't know what would. Pointed the camera, pushed the button. But just at the very moment when I began to pan the camera left, I heard Mom's anxious-bordering-on-panicked cry.

"Jeremy!"

Another moment and my camera was pointed directly at our five-year-old.

Standing on the wall.

A half step from . . . from . . . well, from very bad things.

I suppose the little guy just wanted an unblocked-by-the-dang-wall view of that river and the magnificent canyon it's been carving since caves were art galleries. And to be honest, in retrospect, I admire and envy the courage and blatant disregard for life-and-death danger that allowed my boy to hop up onto that wall, without hesitation.

But only in retrospect.

At the time, I felt like every fluid in my body dropped in a heartbeat to sea level and every reflex said adios and disappeared beyond the horizon with shameless speed. But right before the meltdown was complete, I saw Mom reach out and grab the little fella's arm, bringing him off that wall quicker than a John Wayne grimace.

It all took but a moment. But sometimes a moment's all it takes to change lives forever, and we brushed that flame just a tad too close for me. Sometimes I think back and imagine grimly what might've happened had we been farther than an arm's length from our little wall-climbing critter. But I can only entertain that thought for an instant before my repression skills send the horror back to the depths from which it, thankfully, springs only occasionally.

Now, I'd like to tell you that I was calm as a church whisper in the next few minutes after that. I'd like to tell you that, despite the heart-stopping scare he'd inflicted on me, I didn't holler on the boy or show impatience in any degree or accuse him of having less-than-adequate sense.

And I'd probably risk saying all that, hoping that you and everyone else would then think me a most incredibly integrated father.

But the camera was rolling.

***

Don't think those little feet are all that prompts gray hairs on a parent's pate. There's also that little mouth to be dealt with.

I suppose young'uns have managed since the dawn of time to cause some kind of a ruckus with the occasional unexpected or embarrassing or mistimed remark.

I mean, I wasn't there in the beginning of days to know for sure one way or the other, and nothing's recorded in Holy Writ about the doings of Cain and Abel as young'uns. But if you're a parent, I'm sure you can just imagine Father Adam introducing four-year-old Cain to the neighbor—there must have been one, no?—from the other side of the mountain and hearing Cain blurt out to the stranger, just out of the blue, "My daddy drools and snores."

Just march your little self straight to your tent, Cain.

I'm sure it must've been pretty soon after that when somebody issued an edict that children were to be seen and not heard, so probably nobody heard anything else from kids till 1777 when sixteen-year-old Sybil Ludington had that little spat with her father, insisting that he allow her to take a solo forty-mile horseback ride around the New England countryside.

***

When Dianne's parents retired some years ago, they moved from their Placentia, California, home to a new one just a mile or two from ours. We were tickled pink to have them nearby at last. But in the years before they made the move, we were occasionally treated to a visit by them and whichever of Dianne's six siblings were still in the nest. We treasured every visit.

And so it was, one day, that the Raddatz clan came to visit. Anne, Kristopher, and Jeremy were about five years, three years, and one year old, respectively, and they loved—with a capital L—to see Grandma Jo and Grandpa and their uncles and aunt. Before Grandpa's car had come to a full stop in front of our house, the kidlets were already at the front window, squealing with excitement. Car doors flew open and slammed shut, and through the door our welcome visitors poured, lovingly attacked by our trio. Actually, there was a lot of mutual attacking going on—after all, these children represented three-fifths of Grandma's and Grandpa's grandchildren at the time, and they didn't often get their hands on 'em. Lots of squishing and slurpy kisses all around.

It was standard procedure for the beginning of a visit, all this squishing and kissing—and it was invariably followed by "oooohs" and "ahhhhs" and "my goodness, how you've grown." You might see a little body tossed happily into the air amid joyful shrieks and squeals, or some hair tousled here and there—maybe even a hasty bit of peek-a-boo with the littlest. Then the group would move in synchronicity like a flock of starlings or a school of clown loaches, with maneuver waves steering the whole bunch in graceful unison to the living room for continued hugging and munching and some getting-caught-up.

As soon as the group was seated, grandparents wanted to know all about school and church and birthdays and favorite cartoon characters and whatnot, and the little ones were as happy as a cow on a vegetarian farm to share their news with attentive grandparents, uncles, and aunt.

Good old-fashioned conversation.

When I think about all the icebreakers my little Anne might've tossed into the crossfire that day . . . well, there were many possibilities. So very many. I mean, even at the tender age of five, she might've thought to say something about her kindergarten teacher or the kid who sat next to her in the classroom or what glue-and-glitter project she'd just finished. She might've hinted at what she hoped to see under the tree, come Christmas, or whether she'd be a witch or a princess or Winnie the Pooh at Halloween. She might've bragged about a new toy or told how her brothers had been so naughty or explained why she preferred pizza to eggplant.

Or she might've mentioned our bedtime fun. Horsey-back rides to the bedroom. Stories from a grand library of kiddie books—read with made-up voices, intentional errors for the kids to catch and laugh about, and hand gestures to describe the action. Funny little games with bed sheets pulled taut over chins, playful taps on the head with a paperback book in feigned aggravation, drinks of water till the cows came home, now-I-lay-me-down-to-sleeps.

So many wonderful thoughts my sweet daughter might've thrown into the conversation.

But she didn't go for any of those things. Apparently she'd had something on her mind for the longest time and had been waiting for precisely the right moment to share it with the world.

And this, I guess, was that moment.

"My daddy picks his nose."

It was one of those times when a daddy feels that special kind of pride in his young'uns and wants the whole wide world to know he's had a hand in their upbringing.

Now, I'm not gonna comment one way or the other on the accuracy of Anne's observation. I'm not even claiming the right to fifth-amendment protection because that's just a fancy way of saying, "I did it, but I'm not gonna tell on myself."

I say only this: let him who is without . . . well, you know the rest.

***

In the Morris household, sit-down meals were mandatory. None of this grab-a-plate-and-head-for-the-TV stuff for us.

The children knew our meals were cooked in the kitchen and served at the table. They knew they had to at least sample every single item on the menu—and unless that nibble caused some horrible reaction that hinted of death or disability, they'd eat everything that was put on that pretty white Corelle plate. They knew they had to remain at the table till everyone finished eating. And they knew that they were allowed to leave the table only after they'd asked to be excused and thanked their mother for the lovely meal.

In today's world, some would argue that Dianne and I should be brought up on charges for making our children do such things—and others—that they didn't necessarily always wanna do. But make no mistake: I'd risk those charges if I were raising children today because the upside to that kind of routine and structure's pretty big.

One evening, we were sitting at the table, enjoying some of the best home cooking this side of . . . well, of *any*where, because my children's mama can cook. Oh, yeah. You can bet your lifetime Weight Watchers membership on it. Our six-year-old Kristopher had come to the table with contraband of some kind or another and his occupation with it was interfering just a tad with the family moment.

See, we not only ate meals at the dinner table every day, but we also actually spoke between bites. We found it to be a good way to stay in touch with one another and know a little something about the people we were sharing a house with.

On a related note, this table was also where the youngsters learned manners and etiquette, things that are too often strange notions to kids in today's world. Yep, our three got to learn what a napkin's for and how to use it. They learned a proper place setting, how to use a knife and a fork and a spoon, and how to politely ask for something to be passed and wait for it to get to them. Heck, they even learned to take off their hats while they ate.

Anyway, Kristopher's fiddling with this whatever-it-was seemed to be short-circuiting our communication a bit. Asking him to surrender it seemed the right thing to do, so I asked. With a short ration of glum, he handed it over.

Now, anyone who knows me will find it terribly difficult to believe, but in those days it wasn't completely unheard of for me to get the slightest bit snippy from time to time.

This is where I'd roll my eyes and clear my throat ironically if I were telling the story instead of writing it.

I can't remember clearly—effective repression, probably—but I suppose this must have been one of those times. I took the thing from Kristopher, opened the door to the carport—it was just to my left, as I sat at the south end of the table—and tossed the confiscated treasure past the concrete steps that led into the house. Now, I didn't break anything, mind you, and no animals were harmed in the process, but given Kristopher's reaction, I guess I must've sent that thing out of the house with a bit of energy.

"Well, *^#!*, Dad, you don't have to just *throw* it!"

Hmmm.

I looked at Mom. Mom looked at me. Eyebrows raised, jaws dropped, and then two sets of eyes went to Kristopher, in concert.

"What did you say, son?" You know, just to be sure. Heck, maybe we hadn't really heard what we thought we'd heard.

He repeated, without a blink.

"Well, *^#!*, Dad, you don't have to just *throw* it!"

Hmmm, in spades.

***

You can find just all kinds of psychology floating around this world, some of it good and some of it not so good—and with undergraduate and graduate degrees in the field, I suppose I've been exposed to most of it. Structuralism, functionalism, behaviorism, and a few *isms* I can't remember. Psychoanalysis, behavior modification, operant conditioning, classical conditioning, person-centered therapy, and rational emotive behavior therapy. Natural consequences. Logical consequences. Reflective listening. Positive reinforcement, negative reinforcement, time out, punishment—and, no, negative reinforcement and punishment are *not* the same thing. Differential reinforcement of incompatible behavior. Differential reinforcement of other behavior. Differential reinforcement of lower rates of behavior.

Then, of course, there are traditional parenting techniques, which are really just translations of high-brow terms into the more routine blue-collar terms we know so well: yelling, pleading, scolding, threatening, bullying, cajoling, spanking, grounding, promising, bribing, ignoring.

I mean, there are just a quadrabatrillion possible ways of responding to things your kids do.

And everybody and his dog has a notion—backed by clinical or empirical or anecdotal data, of course—about what makes humans tick and what we should all do with or to or for each other to get along in this life.

But despite countless lectures, books, papers, discussions, internships, externships, practica, and exams, I guess I never fully decided just which school of thought or methodology was really my thing. In jobs as a psychologist at the Training School and in the public school system, and as an administrator in public and private venues, I've used it all, in one way, shape, or form. But even now, in the winter of my professional life, I still don't know exactly which school of thought or methodology I favor.

Perhaps we'll just call my thinking *eclectic.*

Listening to my eldest son's first . . . first . . . well, I was gonna say first *swear* word, but it wasn't that. Not really. And it wasn't a curse. It wasn't obscene or vulgar or dirty or disgusting.

It was simply inappropriate. Well, maybe not so *simply*, but inappropriate.

Anyway, hearing my son say that word, however you categorized it, I intuitively knew that nothing I'd learned or accepted or rejected or argued or thought about psychology, or any method I'd used in the practice of same, could help me at that moment. I figured I should probably *do something*, but not a single cubic centimeter in my fatherly cranium was available for any thought of disciplining or punishing or yelling. It all seemed suddenly perfectly pointless.

The moment was funny, plain and simple. And that's all there was to it.

Mom and I taught briefly, but we didn't make a big deal of the episode. We couldn't—it took everything we had just to muffle the chuckles, trying to keep the boy from getting the idea that it'd be OK for him to say that word whenever I chucked something out of the house.

I guess we handled it all right, because to this very day, having known that young man for thirty-four terrific years, I've never heard him say that word again, ever—in the wrong context.

In fact, after writing this memory, I tried to remember the last time I heard him say *any* inappropriate word in anger or frustration.

I couldn't think of a time.

I went to his mother and asked her to try to remember.

She couldn't think of a time.

I went to his older sister and younger brother and asked them too.

They couldn't think of a time.

I guess he got it all out of his system at the dinner table that night.

***

This daddy thing's kinda ironic.

What daddies need at the beginning of the gig is what they can have only at the end of it, after having picked it up a piece at a time over the years.

Wisdom.

Yeah, that little treasure comes only with time and lots of experience. And attention.

Teaching children to face and manage stairs properly, Dad may see the wisdom in helping them face and manage other life challenges similarly. If he chases enough bikes, he may learn about proper balance between holding on and letting go. With a scare or two, he may understand that there are times when, no matter how much independence is allowed a child, being within an arm's reach can be a good thing. And treated to the honesty and innocence of a child's poorly selected words, he may discover that a simple smile is sometimes the best psychology of all.

So many metaphors, so little time.

SIX

BATTLES AND PIANO LESSONS

con·flict (v. kən·flikt; n. kon·flikt), v.i. 1. to come into collision or disagreement; be contradictory, at variance, or in opposition; clash. 2. to fight or contend; do battle. 3. a fight, battle, or struggle, esp. a prolonged struggle; strife. 4. controversy; quarrel. 5. discord of action, feeling, or effect; antagonism or opposition, as of interests or principles. 6. striking together; collision. — Syn. 1. collide, oppose. 3. encounter, siege. See fight. 5. contention, opposition. — Ant. 4. accord.

As a new father, I was interested in the experiences of veteran fathers. I figured if I paid careful attention to what these blooded patriarchs could tell me, I'd turn out like Ward Cleaver or Jim Anderson or Mike Brady or Howard Cunningham—or some other perfect TV dad. Yep, I'd know the right answer to every question and the proper plan for every circumstance, and I'd make things perfectly clear to the confused kid—every time.

Sometimes, I got good help and advice from the vets.

But if I had a dollar for every time some frazzled, battle-weary dad warned me that I'd rue the day I fathered a child—"believe you me," they'd usually add—when that child turned thirteen, or even if I had just a quarter for every blood-curdling story about the horrors of having teenagers in the house . . . well, if I did, then I'd have enough dollars and quarters to live royally in some perennially temperate climate.

San Diego, probably.

Sadly, not a single dollar or quarter for any of it. What I did collect, though, was just a whole big *lot* of apprehension about the battles that seemed to be headed my way, sure as Lombardi disliked losing. And when the witching hour was upon us and Anne, our eldest, turned thirteen, I waited with bated breath for her to develop fangs, claws, and body hair and show obsessive-compulsive interest in lunar cycles.

But my anxiety was *way* exaggerated. No werewolves for us. See, what I'd failed to consider as a new, inexperienced father was that teenagers don't just pop out of thin air. Nope, it didn't occur to me that they'd start out as little critters and I'd get a dozen or so years to get to know them as they grew and evolved—and they, me. We'd have tons of time and loads of opportunities to figure things out a bit at a time and evolve a game plan, as it were, all the while building a relationship that'd help stem the trickier tides of adolescence.

Hadn't counted on having a perfect first child, either.

But that's essentially what I had. An obedient, smart, sweet-spirited, easy-to-be-entreated daughter that set the example and showed the way for her younger brothers to follow.

That helped. Oh, yeah. That helped a lot.

So much, in fact, that the proverbial other shoe simply never dropped.

***

Now, don't get me wrong. I'm not saying I never had to go toe-to-toe with a young'un. That'd just be a big fat story. But as we stumbled and marked our way through childhood years together, the children learned lessons, and so did I—lessons that helped us survive the occasional tiff that was inevitable when they began to test the waters of independence and decision-making.

Here's one of the lessons I learned, nicely coined by John James Ingalls:

"Pick battles big enough to matter, small enough to win."[1]

Perhaps it was more a realization or acknowledgment than lesson learned. Whatever it was, it occurred to me that if I insisted on fighting with my kids about every little thing they wanted to do or didn't want to do for the next six or eight years, our family life would feature more conflict than a Hatfield and McCoy barn-raising. Not for me, thank you. Nope, I just flat did *not* wanna fight a major battle every time a child asked to sleep over at a friend's house or move a piece of bedroom furniture to another wall or wear red tennis shoes instead of white ones.

I mean, if a dad looks for them, he can find all kinds of reasons to pick a fight with his children. Heck, young'uns can be a whole lotta stupid sometimes.

But let's just be fair about this thing. When you get right down to it, dads can be just as stupid sometimes.

The trouble is, many men are led to believe—or maybe they just accept the notion, uninfluenced—that a father's job description includes certain essential duties that must never,

ever, *ever* be moderated in the slightest, if the world would continue to spin on its axis.

Examples.

First, a father's gotta carefully scrutinize every single thing his kids do, from rooster's crow till the little troublemakers hit the hay. Second, he's gotta point up every single thing the kidlets do that he doesn't like and tell them to stop it—or, coming at it through the back door, point out every single thing they *aren't* doing that he *wants* them to do and tell them to *do* it. Third, he's gotta threaten his kids with Old Testament wrath if they don't stop what he told them to stop, or don't start what he told them to start. And finally, the *coup de grâce*: Dad's gotta throw down a four-hour monologue in which he tells how he handled this kind of thing when he was young.

Always perfectly, of course. That's how we dads *always* did things when we were kids. Heaven forbid a father should admit to being a sixth-grade cutup or making a dumb decision in high school or getting in trouble at college or simply enjoying a little mischief whenever.

Okay. So I'm being just a tad sarcastic here. Exaggerating a bit too. And while I'm at it, let me just go ahead and admit to over-generalizing as well. That aside, I still believe we dads pick more fights than we should. And it stands to reason that you can't fight with your kids about everything under the sun and expect to live in a home filled with harmony and light. It just ain't happening, Bub. The secret to happiness in a home where children are growing and parents are learning is understanding that not every minor misstep a child takes, or goofy preference a child has, or bad decision a child makes is cause for Gettysburg reenacted.

***

But I can hear you right now, saying, "Okay, Kev, Mister *Perfect*. You must think you were, like, the world's greatest dad."

Uhhhh . . . nope. Quite to the contrary, I'm a graduated student of experience in this thing.

Yep, traveling the roads of daddydom I've made about a gazillion goofs. Shoot, in the early years I made more mistakes than there are mirrors in a Kardashian household. Oh, yeah. I scolded my toddlers for stuff they weren't even aware they'd done. I hollered on my eight-year-olds for things so trivial I couldn't remember three minutes later what the issue'd been. I promised the most awesome biblical plagues and punishments if whatever it was I didn't like didn't stop, *and I mean this instant!* I threatened to *turn this car around and go home* more times than Elvis got kissed. I pounded out hours-long autobiographic soliloquies so painful that my preadolescents, I'm sure, prayed silently for a swift and comprehensive end-of-days scenario. And even if I grew slightly less stupid and gained some positive momentum as years wore on, mistakes never completely stopped. Nor will they, ever. At least that's my best guess.

But with an exception or two, I've somehow managed to beat back the burdensome guilt that the human mind seems determined to inflict on its owner. Because I realized early on that I'd never be that perfect TV father and didn't expect to be, I've never held myself to be a failure just because this thing or that went awry from time to time. Error-prone, to be sure, but never a failure—even when I look back on innumerable mistakes and immeasurable stupidity.

The good news is that I learned from the ill-thought decisions and mistaken judgments and erroneous conclusions and misdirected discipline. Yep, even this dough-headed dad eventually saw the wisdom in restricting the daddy-teen battlefield to manageable perimeters.

***

But it stood to reason that if I was gonna be conservative in the picking of battles with my adolescent children, I'd be obliged to adopt a . . . well, a *corollary*, if you will, to the general philosophy of conservative battle-picking.

Actually, I had to adopt two corollaries. Here's the first:

"War is an ugly thing, but not the ugliest of things: the decayed and degraded state of moral and patriotic feeling which thinks nothing is worth a war, is worse."[2]

And the second:

"Once we have a war, there is only one thing to do. It must be won. For defeat brings worse things than any that can ever happen in war."[3]

Yeah, I know these men were referring to *real* war. The awful kind, where things get exploded and people get eighty-sixed. But in their words lies a veiled truth at least as important as the literal. Take Mr. Hemingway's observation in the second quotation, for example. Whether the writer recognized the metaphor or not, the truth is that there may, in fact, be weighty long-term consequences to be reckoned with when a dad engages a child over something important and then loses the battle.

But that's a thought for another day.

For now, suffice it to say that I adopted the corollaries: some select issues would be worth the battle; and if I was gonna go to the bother of picking that battle, it was gonna be *won*.

Take piano lessons, for example.

***

Now, my children have a talent for music, and over the years they've shown it, each in his or her own way. Through junior high and high school, Anne played the flute, and Kristopher, the trumpet. Jeremy never played a band instrument, but he thought about taking up the Samchillian Tip Tip Tip Cheeepeeeee. Problem was, you couldn't buy one at Summerhays Music in those days. Our youngest mastered the radio in a special way though, and had the innate rhythm of a Brazilian conga drummer at a Cuban bistro. Plus he sang in the odd chorus and whatnot, as did his brother and sister. And none of them fell to the floor a whole lot while dancing.

[*Oldies Note:* My children know more about sixties music than anybody their age—you can bet your classic Garrard turntable on that. In fact, I've heard it's illegal in at least nine states for a thirty-something to know so much about sixties music.]

When I think about it, I see that the young'uns came by such talent rightfully. Seems they were bound to brush against it at least a little—both sides of their DNA kinda insisted on it. Take their mother and me, for example. I'm no Don Ellis or Eric Clapton or Fred Astaire, to be sure, but I've fiddled around with a few instruments and taken a turn or two around the dance floor in my day. As for singing, I usually get more notes right than wrong. And their mom . . . well, Mom's angelic voice will suit heaven's purposes just fine, thank you very much. Plus she handles the ol' eighty-eight well enough. And although it's true that she was kicked out of dance class at the ripe old age of four—for falling over a lot and breaking things, rumor has it—we don't hold that against her.

Dianne and I share family tree limbs with brothers and sisters of remarkable talent, and on the limbs above the two of us hang parents, aunts, uncles, grandparents, and great-grandparents similarly inclined.

Take my maternal grandmother, for instance. Born and raised in rural Mississippi, Mama Hamblin had precious little time to develop any skill or talent that didn't contribute to the basic necessities of a life sustained by hard work. Her weathered hands testified that she was more often required to turn a never-ending chore than allowed to press an ivory-covered piano key.

But make no mistake: she could press an ivory-covered piano key.

This grand lady never took lessons. Never even learned to read music. But using the shaped notes of the Broadman Hymnal, Mama Hamblin taught herself to play hymns on the old, clunky upright in her humble home. And play them beautifully.

Pansy Lee Hickey Hamblin's vita boasted no Carnegie Hall performance, to be sure—but when she sat in for the regular pianist at her church meetings, her hands "moved over the keys like the sun's rays bouncing over water, or blue skies dispelling rain."[4]

I've tried to imagine the potential of this wonderful woman's talent, had she opportunity to study properly, beyond what fate allocated.

***

We were late getting around to piano lessons. Jeremy was ten, Kristopher was thirteen, and Anne was fifteen when we hooked them up. I was principal of a "special placement" public school then, and the music teacher there was a good friend who taught piano on the side. She agreed to give weekly lessons to our brood.

For a time, Margie came to our house and gave each of the little rascals a half hour in turn. After a while, the venue changed to her house. We'd drop the bunch there and then collect them a couple of hours later.

After several weeks, things were moving along nicely. Mostly.

I say *mostly* because Anne and Jeremy seemed to enjoy the lessons and were making good progress. That would be two out of three, and, last I checked, two out of three constituted a majority, so . . . things were going nicely, *mostly.*

Well . . . *enjoy* may be too strong a word. *Tolerate* may be more accurate. But no matter which verb you wanna defend, the upshot was that Anne and Jeremy were at least cooperative with Margie as she tried to pound into them the intricacies of the ivory. They listened respectfully as she pointed up their errors again and again, and they kept a civil tongue, even when they thought Margie was more Bloody Mary than Mary Poppins.

Yep, they just took it politely and kept on hunting middle C.

Kristopher was a different story.

Our second-born began to show a new side to his usually pleasant, friendly, and well-behaved self. He just didn't like this piano thing. He didn't like it, a *lot.* Well, truth be told, his dislike was aimed more at the teacher than at the piano. To say that he wasn't fond of Margie understated the obvious. Partly, this conflict was a matter of personalities and perceptions, as conflicts so often are. Kristopher had an idea of what good piano playing should look and sound like, and Margie had a different idea about it—and they dealt with this disagreement about as nicely as the Jets and the Sharks, except that baseball bats and switchblades never entered into it.

It came close sometimes, though.

If Margie asked Kristopher to play a bit more legato, he'd staccato the heck out of every note he saw. If she insisted on forte, he'd counter with a pianissimo possibile that barely got the hammers to the strings. Allegro? Largo. Presto? Prestissimo.

You get the picture.

And when she'd holler on him for making the same mistake twenty-seven times in a row—usually with a subtle smile on his naughty little face—he'd bark right back with no conscience.

Think of Monty Python's John Cleese and Michael Palin in the famous "Argument Clinic" skit.[5] That mental picture will be right close to what we saw every time Kristopher and Margie sat at the piano together, except that Messieurs Cleese and Palin were hopeless amateurs in the graceful art of argument compared to this teacher and student.

And when he wasn't sharing the bench with Margie, Kristopher's attitude about piano larnin' wasn't any better. I mean, sure . . . he'd practice once in a while, if I threatened to remove his lungs through his nose. But even when such bullying actually got him to the piano, you'd seldom hear more than three notes during the half hour, and two of them would be wrong.

Piano lessons in the Morris household looked like this for some time: Anne and Jeremy were cooperative and polite, while Kristopher practiced passive-aggression, mastered the art of the insult, and devised twenty-seven new facial expressions to convey boredom, hostility, resistance, and disgust.

For Kristopher, the whole piano project was perfectly pointless. He wanted nothing to do with it, found joy neither in practice nor performance, and wanted with all his willful little heart to rip the soundboard from the piano, burn the bench, and contrive some incantation to magically transport Margie to the innermost regions of the Sagittarius Dwarf Elliptical Galaxy.

But sometimes life can be such a perfect paradox.

***

After only a year or so of lessons, interest in the fine art of piano waned. Anne was first to bail. At sixteen, she had a variety of other things on her mind and on her agenda, and the lessons and practice time were beginning to get in the way. She let her mother and me know she'd just rather not continue with piano lessons, if we didn't mind.

Dianne and I talked about it. We felt no urge to argue.

That was the end of piano training for Anne.

Soon Jeremy decided that it wasn't in his best interests to spend all that time on the piano bench. There were sports to be played, you know—and between athletics and music training, he figured a higher return on an investment in athletics.

Dianne and I talked about it. We felt no urge to argue.

That was the end of piano training for Jeremy.

When Kristopher saw the others drop like flies, he was encouraged. He figured to be the final dropout, bringing an end to Margie's attempted coup of the Morris household. Hopeful, he approached his mother and me to suggest that this piano thing was no more important for him than for Anne and Jeremy. "Maybe we should just make this next lesson the last," he suggested.

He had tennis, he reminded us. And band, he reminded us. And a gazillion other irons in the fire, he reminded us.

Dianne and I talked about it.

Dianne and I thought about it.

Dianne and I puzzled about it.

We felt a distinct urge to argue.

And argue we did. For his part, Kristopher actually put forth a rather convincing case, truth be told.

Perhaps you've enjoyed the following scene from the 1992 film *My Cousin Vinny.*

Vinny's a last-in-his-class attorney in the courtroom for the first time, defending his cousin and a friend against a charge of murder. To say the least, he hasn't made a good impression on Judge Haller, who presides. When the district attorney calls a surprise witness, Vinny objects. The judge summons both attorneys to the bench to hear the complaint. Vinny explains.

"I object to this witness being called at this time," Vinny says. "We've been given no prior notice he'd testify. No discovery of any tests he's conducted or reports he's prepared. And as the court is aware, the defense is entitled to advance notice of any witness who will testify, particularly to those who will give scientific evidence, so that we can properly prepare for cross-examination, as well as to give the defense an opportunity to have the witness's reports reviewed by a defense expert, who might then be in a position to contradict the veracity of his conclusions."

"Mr. Gambini?" says Judge Haller, looking a bit surprised.

"Yes, sir?" Vinny answers.

"That is a lucid, intelligent, well thought-out objection."

"Thank you, Your Honor."

"Overruled."[6]

Kristopher fared no better with his objection.

Mom and Dad were confident in our decision. We were firm in our commitment. Somehow, we were certain of a favorable outcome.

"Son, you've just gotta trust us on this thing," I told Kristopher. "It's not the right thing for you to quit. We're sure of it."

And then, without hesitation or conscience, I laid on this young man that most-repeated parent promise. That most-used parent prophecy. That blue ribbon-winning, cake-taking, if-it's-been-said-once-it's-been-said-a-million-times parent cliché.

"One day you'll thank us for this, son."

Of course, Kristopher understood our point of view perfectly, after we discussed this thing for a while. He recognized that we were only discharging our responsibility as parents. He accepted our judgment and agreed with each point we made. Heck, he was just flat tickled pink about this.

Not.

By week's end, we'd seen every single one of those twenty-seven facial expressions he'd devised to convey boredom, hostility, resistance, and disgust.

And throw in two or three new ones, for anger.

Never mind. We'd made our decision. Unsure why, Dianne and I agreed that this was a battle worth fighting. And we knew it would be a battle in nearly every sense of the word, and bloody—for a time, anyway. But we cemented our alliance in this thing and determined to stand firm, no matter what.

And now I had another fight on my hands. One I hadn't anticipated, although I probably should've.

***

"Kevin, I'm sorry, but I just can't be Kristopher's teacher any longer."

That's what Margie told me at school one day.

Then she elaborated.

"I mean, he's obstinate, negative, disobedient, sarcastic, stubborn, uninterested, and . . . well, I could go on but I think you get the picture. I dread every single lesson. I'd rather be strapped to Sing Sing's Old Sparky than sit on the piano bench with Kris."

Bummer.

Yeah, we could've found another teacher, certainly. But

no matter what Kristopher thought of Margie, we knew she was good at her work. She'd already endured a considerable amount of misery, so we figured . . . well, heck. She could probably endure a little more. And because she followed the rigid requirements of the National Guild of Piano Teachers, we knew she'd teach our son properly.

Ironically, this Guild was probably the very thing that drove a wedge between Margie and Kristopher. While she subscribed to its exacting standards for technique and performance, our son preferred to play outside the lines, so to speak. He *felt* music every bit as much as he *read* music—even more, truth be told. And while teacher was harping on hand position and posture, student was given more and more to interpretation.

Which, by the way, may have been the very reason why his mother and I sensed a need to insist that Kristopher continue this piano thing.

Perhaps he didn't simply have talent.

Perhaps he had The Gift.

Gift or no, we would suffer a terrible setback here, we thought, if Margie quit and we had to break in a new sucker . . . I mean, teacher. We worried about all that frying-pan-and-fire stuff.

So . . . I begged. "Just a little more time, Margie," I said. "You can't deny he's got talent," I challenged. "We'll do everything we can to get him on the page with you," I promised.

Maybe this battle-weary instructor saw the sincerity in my eyes or heard the desperation in my voice. Perhaps she was emotionally defenseless against my eloquence—which was no doubt marvelous—and had no choice but to give in. Could be she was visionary and imagined the Frederic Chopin or George Gershwin or Liberace or Barry Manilow or Elton John that would come of her super-heroic effort.

I strongly doubt that Margie's response had anything to do with the fact that I was her boss and could make her workday seem like a work*month*, if I'd a mind to.

Whatever the reason, Margie agreed to continue the lessons . . . or *torture*, as she put it.

***

For a while, there was precious little change, if any. Lessons were still all kinds of horrible, for student and teacher. Kristopher still didn't wanna be where he was when he was on that bench, and Margie still hoped for a general anesthesia to get her through the half hour. The Morris household was still a battleground every day around practice time.

And then one of Kristopher's best friends, who was taking piano lessons too, introduced Kristopher to a pianist whose music our struggling young artist found interesting. In this newly discovered musician's style, our son saw a similarity to the mental picture he'd held and vigorously defended through all the technique imposed on him by Margie and the Guild.

David Lanz, the pianist. "Cristofori's Dream," the piece.[7]

Before you could say, *Don't bother me; I'm practicing*, Kristopher had that little gem memorized. He played it skillfully, with the emotion that had been struggling so long to find the light of day. He played as though he'd composed the piece himself and knew the true meaning behind each note.

It was beautiful.

And Kristopher's soul was exposed.

From that moment, we couldn't keep the boy away from the dang piano. He'd discovered the enjoyment he'd so carefully denied and the talent he'd so willfully resisted, and now he couldn't get enough of what he was able to produce.

Margie moved away not long after. Word had it she checked herself into a rehab facility of some kind for two or three years of rest and decompression. After she left us, we never engaged another teacher, but Kristopher didn't really need one. You couldn't stop him from playing or progressing. And soon he'd discover that he had not only the talent to make a piano purr, but also a gift for composition. In a style as comfortable as a light summer breeze wafting over a mirror-still lake, he effortlessly crafted pieces that expressed what he felt, in the way he'd always wanted to express it. Family, friends, passersby, any lost travelers who found themselves by chance in our neighborhood—all were drawn to that sound like kids to puppies.

At nineteen years of age, Kristopher agreed to give two years of volunteer service. He'd soon learn that something special was waiting there for him.

***

Kristopher was assigned to work with a fellow volunteer who, as it turned out, was of like talent. The two soon discovered their mutual love for music, and before you could say, *It's music to my ears*, they were combining their talents. With Kristopher at the piano and the two of them singing, the pair traveled about, presenting an inspired and beautiful message. The makeup of the audience didn't matter. Nope, wherever they presented, the result was the same: The music encouraged in the listener a spirit of love and service. It touched the hearts of many. It changed the lives of many.

Kristopher wrote a letter to his mother and me each week throughout the two years of service. Reading those letters, it wasn't uncommon for a tear to glisten its way down my cheek. The words of a young man immersed in service to others tapped tender emotions, often. In addition to the letters, we enjoyed personal phone calls from time to time.

It was during one such phone call that we heard what we'd hoped for.

"Thanks, Mom and Dad, for making me take piano lessons and not giving up on me."

In a flash I recalled the disagreements, the arguments, the frustrations, the battles of piano lessons. But those bleak images didn't linger. Swift to replace them was the satisfying vision of what our son had achieved and, more important, what he'd found in himself.

Yes, we chose to fight this battle with Kristopher. It wasn't pretty, for a while. At times, his mother and I weren't sure whether we were winning or losing. And there were wounds, but they healed—what came of the struggle was worth every metaphorical drop of blood.

Sometimes, in those sober moments of reflection that stand peacefully between the done and the doing, I look back on the battles Dianne and I chose to engage and the ones we passed on, and wonder how many times we chose badly. I suppose it's only human, this second-guessing oneself, and surely I can't be the only father that ever wondered how this thing or that might've turned out if he'd behaved differently at some crossroads moment. I can hope only for a respectable lifetime batting average, knowing it's likely that I swung badly more than once.

No matter. It all seems to have come out in the wash. And today, when I see my son at the piano with his children, encouraging them to discover their own gifts, I know that one battle, anyway, was chosen well.

NOTES

1. John James Ingalls (1833–1900), US senator from Kansas (1873–1891), for whom a peer suggested this epitaph: "Up was he stuck, and in the very upness of his stuckitude he fell." I'd give a nickel to have written that.

2. John Stuart Mill (1806–1873), British philosopher, economist. "The Contest in America," *Dissertations and Discussions* (1859). Written to oppose England's siding with the Confederacy during the American Civil War.

3. Ernest Hemingway, ed., *Men at War* (New York: Crown Publishers, 1942), Brimhall Edition, 1979, xi.

4. Robert Hamblin, "Mama at the Piano," *Crossroads: Poems of a Mississippi Childhood* (St. Louis: Time Being Books, 2010), 55.

5. Michael Palin, John Cleese, Graham Chapman, Eric Idle, Terry Jones, and Rita Davies, "The Argument Clinic" or "The Argument Sketch," *Monty Python's Flying Circus*, episode 29, written by John Cleese and Graham Chapman, aired November 2, 1972.

6. *My Cousin Vinny*, directed by Jonathan Lynn (Los Angeles: 20th Century Fox, 1992).

7. David Lanz, "Cristofori's Dream," *Cristofori's Dream*, (Glendale, WI: Narada, 1988).

SEVEN

WHAT-IFS AND WORTH-ITS

For all its difficulty and haphazardness, there's simply nothing to match the daddy thing for joy, learning, growth, fun, and value. From the point of view of this particular daddy, anyway, it's a most wonderful ride that shouldn't be missed, by choice.

I mean, yeah, it's a lot of hard work, this raising kids. And it grows gray hairs. And sometimes you've gotta take a Tums.

You've gotta deal with diapers and baby food and bike riding and close calls. Teenager angst. Pimples. Self-image. Homework. Piano lessons. The broken this and the sprained that.

You've gotta be Solomon except that you only get to be right part of the time—and when you're wrong, you're *big* wrong.

There's no money in it, either. That's for dang sure. Most of the time, in fact, money flies out of the ol' piggy bank faster than lame-duck presidents pardon felons.

Okay. I've convinced myself. I should never have done it.

No, wait.

Come to think of it, it's all turned out pretty nice.

***

Once, before I got old, fat, and gray, I called my dad to wish him a happy Father's Day. We spoke casually for several minutes and then I got down to brass tacks. I told Dad how much I loved him, how proud I was of him, how glad I'd always been that he's my father. I thanked him for the countless wonderful things he'd done for me. I thanked him for the good memories.

I think I even offered him a dollar for his trouble, but he didn't take it.

Dad's response puzzled me then—but now, years and children and grandchildren later, I think I know why he said what he said.

"I appreciate that, son, but to tell the truth, I've made so many mistakes as a father that it's hard for me to see the dad you're talking about."

That's what he said.

Call it nature, if you will, or a divine plan or simple neurology or complex dynamics of personal relationships or the random kindness of a loving Universe. Call it what you'd like. Whatever it is, there seems to be something that allows children to see and remember the good in a daddy, even when Daddy can't see or remember it himself.

I'm not naive. I understand that there are father-child relationships that resist humorous or loving perspective, even years and years after the child's grown and gone. My heart goes out to any such, because I believe both father and child in that case missed out on a relationship that can be near the top of the *Most Wonderful Relationships in Life* list.

And in every father-child relationship, there are high points and low. When I think back on all I've done as a father, I remember countless wonderful moments with my children, and I treasure them. Every single one of them. But I also have to account for moments when I was less than I ought to have been as a father, and I regret them. Every single one of them.

Thank goodness children don't always remember everything Dad remembers.

I've listened to my children talk among themselves about younger years, flinging memories back and forth like discuses in L. Jay Sylvester's backyard. On Father's Day and birthdays and other special occasions, they've given me cards with handwritten notes that reflect what they've carried in their hearts and heads through the years. They've blogged about their memories. Occasionally, I've even flat-out asked them what they remember of their youth. Yep, I've thrown down that memory gauntlet, bit the bullet, faced the music, let the chips fall.

Give me a second, and I'll come up with another two or three idioms or mixed metaphors to make my dang point.

And let me tell you something. It's gutsy to ask an adult child to rate you as a father. Kinda like dropping trou in Grand Central Station.

But I've done it. Asked the kids, that is—not dropped trou at Grand Central Station. And I'm gonna share with you some of what they've told or written to me.

***

This is risky, I know. If I report weakness, I risk criticism of my skills as a father. If I report success, I risk criticism for pride and vanity. If I report *any*thing, I risk legal action.

I mean, even your own kids can get ticked off and lawyer up.

So I just won't identify which kid wrote or said what.

Here we go.

"My first memory that comes to mind is waiting for my dad to come home from work. I used to LOVE reaching into his coat pocket and finding the Tart 'n' Tiny candy! But asking me to pick a favorite memory of my dad is like asking him to pick his favorite Beatles song. It's just too tough. I do know that my memory and life are full of more positive and meaningful memories than one child deserves. Having said all of that, maybe the most important memory is knowing that I was LOVED every minute of every day of my life."

"It is impossible for me to narrow my favorite memory down to just one. While there are literally hundreds of memories that make me grateful, here are just a few that always remind me of how lucky I am: horsey-back rides with your belt tied around you for me to hold on to ~ tickling your feet with a hair brush ~ having you as Jr. Jazz coach ~ you never missing a single athletic event. Ever. ~ buying my musical instruments and believing that I could actually not only learn how to play them, but play them with feeling, not just how it's written ~ the countless symphony and band concerts you attended ~ hours of football and baseball catch in the front yard and letting me pitch to you even though your knees were sore from the night before ~ hours of 'garbage can basketball' with the Jazz trash can ~ proofreading all my English assignments and helping me diagram sentences ~ selling me your Montero, knowing how much you loved that car ~ providing me everything I needed to get a good education ~ being with me at important events of my life ~ holding my children on the day each was born and asking them 'who loves you?' ~ being a Pappy to my kids ~ being an example to me ~ Sunday dinners ~ the fact that you probably already 'have a chapter about this in your book' ~ being my dad."

"Some words that come to mind when I think of Dad: Gary Puckett ~ cherry chocolates ~ friend ~ channel surfer ~ green Toyota ~ Training School ~ dad ~ trivia ~ writer ~ son ~ listener ~ books ~ records ~ example ~ Pappy ~ pasta maker ~ sweatshirts ~ 'for crying out Pete's sake!' ~ Utah Jazz ~ guitar ~ tennis ~ music ~ Moon Pies ~ leader ~ inspiration ~ tennis shoes ~ David O. McKay ~ Dr. Pepper ~ books ~ Cosmo ~ Murphy's Law ~ crossword puzzles ~ M*A*S*H ~ Robert Frost ~ movies ~ poems ~ BYU ~ office ~ educator ~ Beatles ~ Winger's wings ~ turntables ~ husband ~ funny ~ 'smartest man I know' ~ Germany ~ blue ~ 'I've got a chapter in my book about that' ~ brother ~ Home Alone ~ Dat ~ love ~ family."

***

Well, reviewing what I wrote, I see that it may look like I'm tooting some kind of a horn here. And I can just hear you saying, "Wow, Kev, you've gotta have just about the most inflated ego of anyone since Elvis at the prom." It's a free country, and you're welcome to think that if you like. I already said I knew this would be risky.

Worth the risk, though, 'cause I see something important lurking amidst the memories of my grown-up kidlets.

I mean, just check out how many *little* things they remember. Most of their memories are of little things here and there that I probably didn't think twice about. And they've carried those things with them all these years. Hmmm. Interesting. Maybe there's more to this daddy thing than we like to admit—or even think about. Yeah, our primary job as fathers may be to protect and provide, but it may well be that our involvement in the details of their young lives is what makes the greatest and most lasting impact on them.

As for whatever accolades my children may have generously showered on their dear old dad's gray head as they wrote, don't think for a minute that I don't know what's really at the bottom of all those good memories of theirs.

I do.

The truth is, every good thing our children enjoyed in their youth and everything that's good in them now can be blamed on one person, and only one.

Their mother.

See, for the most part our children came into this world hardwired for good. Whatever finishing touches were required came from Mom. The only thing I can take credit for, really, is not wrecking everything.

I suppose the absence of a negative is a positive. So I'll take credit for that.

What my children graciously omitted from their lists of memories were the *other* times. Times when their dad spoke before thinking and hurt tender feelings. Times when he punished instead of listening and understanding. Times when he wasn't what he should've been.

I can't imagine that I'm the only father who remembers such things and wishes they weren't there for him to remember. But I try not to dwell on those thoughts. What's done is done, and no amount of review or regret or wishing for do-overs can change what's been. Just as I suppose most fathers might say, "I did my best along the way, considering who I was at any given time. I tried to learn. I moved on."

Oh, I'm not trying to be sickeningly humble or self-effacing in this thing—I've contributed a good thing or two to the raising of our children. Most of it by accident, but I contributed. And despite the many mistakes of my daddy-in-training years, it still feels like I've enjoyed the most marvelous ride imaginable in this life—and at every turn I've been better and happier for having taken it.

And thank heaven for that nature or divine plan or neurology or random kindness of a loving Universe that allows children to see and remember the good in a daddy, even when Daddy can't see or remember it himself.

Yes, I know now why Dad said what he said to me on that long-ago Father's Day. But I'm just selfish enough to be glad that my children don't understand that principle any better now than I did then.

EPILOGUE

WHEN THE NEST IS EMPTY

Life has a way of coming full circle.

After all the highways and byways and ups and downs and joys and heartaches of parenting, it seems that life wants to come down, finally, to one relationship. The same relationship that was there first.

Yep, after the children have flown the nest, only two people remain. The same two that started this whole thing.

When our family was preparing for Anne's marriage a few years ago, things were a bit busy around the house, to say the least. Kids going here, Mom running there. Mailing lists and RSVPs. Choosing flowers and menus at The Bungalow. Shopping trips to Mr. Mac's for dark suits. Important religious ceremonies. Cocker Spaniels begging at the fridge. Dad ducking everything he could. Yep, things were hopping. Even the regular sit-down mealtimes we'd taken great care to protect through the years were being sacrificed at the altar of chaos.

One evening near the peak of busy-ness, we all managed to find a seat at the dinner table at the same time. Our youngest,

Jeremy—who might easily have found himself feeling resentful for being excluded from much of the activity that involved only his brother and sister, but hadn't—spoke seriously from across the table.

"Mom. Dad. Things have been kinda busy around here lately, and it seems like the two of you are spending a lot of time by yourselves, without us kids around. Are you OK? Are you handling it OK?"

First let me just say how my heart swelled with pride knowing that the youngest of our children had been sensitive to this matter and bothered to ponder it. Not only that, but the maturity revealed in such empathy was nothing short of wonderful. Not just wonderful, but surprising—considering the maturity level of the father who lent the boy his DNA.

Thank heaven his good mother was also a source of DNA.

Identification of relevant DNA notwithstanding, I heard my son's question. I paused for a moment, catching the eye of his mother and seeing a knowing smile draw slowly and subtly across her face. Then I answered.

"Son, you know that your mother and I love you children more than life itself. There's nothing we wouldn't do to protect you or make you happy. We love you, we're proud of you, and we enjoy every single minute we get to be with you. But," I continued, "you've gotta understand that before we had the three of you, your mother and I had each other. We loved being together then, alone. We love being together now, alone. And while we haven't had as much alone time during the past twenty or so years as we had in the first year of marriage, I'm sure we won't have any trouble remembering how we handled it—because, you see," I explained, "your mother and I like each other."

ABOUT THE AUTHOR

J. Kevin Morris enjoyed a rich childhood in the small town of Baldwyn, Mississippi, and moved with his family to Fullerton, California, when he was eleven. After graduating from Troy High School, he began his university studies, taking a bachelor of science in psychology at Brigham Young University and a master of science in school psychology from the University of Utah. His professional career has included work as a psychologist, behavior consultant, public school administrator, and executive director of a nonprofit service agency. He is married to the former Dianne Raddatz, and the two currently make their home in Saratoga Springs, Utah. They are the very proud parents of three and grandparents of nine. Morris is the author of *Strangely Normal: The (Mostly) True Tales of an Incurable Oddball* (Cedar Fort, 2011). Visit his website at www.jkevinmorris.com.

0 26575 11664 9